Born
Out of
Struggle

SUNY series, Praxis: Theory in Action

Nancy A. Naples, editor

Born Out of Struggle

Critical Race Theory, School Creation, and the Politics of Interruption

David Omotoso Stovall

Published by State University of New York Press, Albany

For information, contact State University of New York Press, Albany, NY
www.sunypress.edu

Production, Ryan Morris
Marketing, Fran Keneston

Library of Congress Cataloging-in-Publication Data

Names: Stovall, David.
Title: Born out of struggle : critical race theory, school creation, and the
 politics of interruption / David Omotoso Stovall.
Description: Albany : State University of New York Press, 2016. | Series:
 SUNY series, praxis, theory in action | Includes bibliographical
 references and index.
Identifiers: LCCN 2015005101| ISBN 9781438459134 (hardcover : alk. paper) |
 ISBN 9781438459141 (paperback : alk. paper) | ISBN 9781438459158 (e-book)
Subjects: LCSH: Critical pedagogy—United States. | Racism in
 education—United States. | Education—Social aspects—United States. |
 Discrimination in education—United States. | Social justice—United
 States.
Classification: LCC LC196.5.U6 S88 2016 | DDC 370.11/5—dc23
LC record available at http://lccn.loc.gov/2015005101

10 9 8 7 6 5 4 3 2 1

*This book is dedicated to the communities of
South Lawndale/Little Village (La Villita) and North Lawndale.
May the quest of both communities to coexist under one roof
in a high school serve as evidence for the
possibility of community justice in Chicago.*

Contents

Foreword

Patricia Maria Buenrostro, *huelgista*,
mother of Greater Lawndale Little Village School
of Social Justice (SOJO) graduate, math educator, and Ph.D. candidate

Carolina Gaete, *huelgista*,
mother of Greater Lawndale Little Village School
of Social Justice student, community organizer

Struggle from the Outside-In: Joining Movements for Change

In January 2001, I was approached by Tomás Gaete to join a group of
Little Village parents working together to investigate the whereabouts and
the whatabouts of a new high school previously promised by the then-
mayor of Chicago, Richard M. Daley. I had recently begun to teach in
a neighboring community and was feeling the need to reconnect to my
hood—so I agreed to attend one of their meetings. Tomás was the community organizer working with the parents and the father of several dear
friends of mine. At this first meeting, I was immediately impressed by the
fact that the parents determined and facilitated the agenda. In my previous short stint in community organizing, I knew this was rare, as many
organizers try to steer the agenda from their perspective to such things as
"winnable" issues and leadership training. This was not the case here. Parents on the west side of Little Village had a long-standing need for a new
high school and wanted answers to an unfulfilled promise and the resulting
misallocation of state funds originally slated for Little Village High School.
The parents with the support of the lead community organization had been

fervently organizing for some time delegations to the Board of Education meetings, even serenading one with a Mariachi, Mexican style. In this first meeting I attended, the parents' determination was palpable, so I decided to join their efforts. Over the next several months, we continued holding accountability sessions for district officials, community summits, and various stakeholder meetings—all in the effort to get answers from the district on the missing funds and to simultaneously draw in more community voices into the conversation. After months of meetings and circular conversations and unanswered questions, we became disillusioned in our fight. It was four days before Mother's Day when we sat in the organization's small, cramped office with long faces and weary hearts. The organization's director, looking at our disheartened wills, threw out the idea of holding a hunger strike on Mother's Day. "Mothers Hungry for an Education" would be the headline. It seemed sensational enough for media outlets to pick it up and get us coverage on Sunday evening news. While we all considered and debated the idea, some immediately ruled it out while others of us considered it for the moment. We had to go back to our families and discuss the implications of launching such a strike. I was one of only four who originally committed to the idea. We came back together on that Saturday to get prepped for the press and by the end of the press conference on Sunday evening, sixteen community residents had committed to carrying out the hunger strike. I myself thought, "How long could this really last? Three days? Five days max?" And so we began to set up camp on the site, putting up tents, requesting a porta-potty on site from the alderman, gathering wood for a campfire. May in Chicago can still be rather chilly. The first few days were awkward and scary as onlookers questioned our presence. Yet it was quite fascinating how quickly a group of people can muster up a collective sense of agency when your next meal is on the line. We marched through the community to inform Little Village residents of our common plight. We formed committees to deal with such things as media, health issues, flyers, and so on. We hosted a wide variety of events on Camp Cesar Chavez from teach-ins to spoken-word events to a community-wide mass to an intimate meeting with Paul Vallas (CEO of Chicago Public Schools at the time) inside a tent on a hot May day. What can I say, Chicago weather can be quite erratic. Most importantly during our nineteen days of strike, we followed the Mayor wherever we knew he would be speaking publicly to interrupt his day, his media coverage, and to remind him that we wanted to know the whereabouts of our money. We interrupted a midday press conference with then–California governor Gray Davis and made the five o'clock news. We interrupted his speaking engagement at a UNO Parents

First educational conference and made the Saturday evening news. And when we couldn't find him in public, we went to his house to interrupt his family dinner. A critical moment was when on May 23, we showed up with hundreds of community residents and supporters to the Board of Education Meeting demanding an answer to the missing $30 million the State of Illinois had specifically allocated for our school. It was only a few days after this meeting that then-CEO Paul Vallas and board president Gery Chico resigned from their posts, as they both had their political gaze set on their upcoming and failed runs to become governor of Illinois. It was a busy nineteen days that our strike lasted. I personally learned a lot about how our city government works and the power of community agency when our target is clear and our commitment is undying. I must acknowledge as many of us did during and after the strike, our victory was *only* possible because of the outpouring of support within Little Village and across the City of Chicago. It was this support that gave us our fuel to continue to fight for and demand justice. This momentous event serves as a reminder of the importance and the right to a quality education our community deserves and fights for daily in both small and big ways.

Fast-forward nine years and my firstborn son enters the doors of the Greater Lawndale Little Village School of Social Justice (or SOJO for short) to begin high school. He is scheduled to graduate in just a few short days from the writing of this foreword. As a parent of a soon to be SOJO graduate, four years ago I had hoped for my son to receive a quality (i.e., rigorous) education, grounded in a culturally and socially relevant curriculum. I hoped that what he was studying actually mattered to him as a socially conscientious youth, while preparing him with the necessary skills to become a successful college graduate. As a young person in a wheelchair, I had hoped that his teachers and the administration would be sensitive and accommodating to his special physical and sometimes academic needs. As a future leader, I had hoped the curriculum writ large would serve to motivate and inspire him to learn and investigate and act on his local context to bring about personal and social change. I had seen how the founding principal and founding teachers had successfully done this with the first graduating class and was anxious for my son to be a part of it.

It's been an honest struggle over the past four years. In his time at SOJO, we have gone through three changes in administration, but fortunately the staff in many ways has held it together. I have incredible respect and love for SOJO teachers, who continue to commit their time and dedication to our students and their growing appetite social justice. I know intimately their own struggles trying to survive in Chicago Public Schools with their frequent administration changes and corresponding mandates and top-down policies. As a parent and community resident, I have tried to do my part but the need to do more is ever present and ever pressing. Prior to my son's entrance, I worked with founding math teachers on their math and social justice curriculum, organized a campuswide student delegation to New Orleans post-Katrina, and even taught a Summer Bridge program for incoming freshman. I served on the local school council and organized with parents to hold the network accountable for removing our democratically elected principal. This fight, of course, was sparked by a student-led protest on the second day of school and ended with the community, once again, speaking out against an injustice followed by the eventual reinstatement of our principal. As you can see, my heart and soul is riding on this little school that could, that has, and that shall, as I have a five-year-old and a seven-month-old who I hope one day will walk through these doors as well. It takes a village to raise a child, and I try to do my part. Even as my son graduates, I will continue to participate on the local school council in order to preserve our history and determine our future. As the students continue to proclaim, "We were born out of struggle and the struggle continues!"

Struggle from the Inside-Out: Sustaining Movements

Walking down the bridge on Thirty-First Street between Kostner and Cicero Avenues, overseeing Camp Cesar Chavez on a rainy, cold, and cloudy May afternoon, feeling as gloomy as the weather, I was fighting and praying with every fiber of my being not to be infested with the venomous feelings of defeat and doubt. I stopped for a while to take in the sight of a wet, empty campsite and wondered if what we had kicked off on Mother's Day was a mistake. With no end in sight, maintaining strength and focus while being ignored and disrespected by Mayor Daley and CPS was becoming very challenging.

From a distance, I could hear very faint chanting but did not see where it was coming from; my first thought was, "Oh Lord, here comes UNO" (United Neighborhood Organization—a community organization politically aligned with the democratic machine) and their cronies to protest our efforts. As the chanting became clearer and louder, I heard, "El pueblo unido jamas sera vencido!" (The people united will never be defeated!), and my mood instantly changed. Over one hundred women in long skirts, children, and men were marching from their parish, La Luz del Mundo (the Light of the World) a Pentecostal church eight blocks away from the

campsite. Overwhelmed by emotion, with tears of joy and gratitude running down my cheeks, I began to run down the bridge as fast as I could
to greet and thank them for giving me a *huge* push of reassurance when
doubt was kicking in. Their prayers and energy injected me with hope and
faith. That moment significantly impacted my understanding of what Poder
Popular (Popular Power) looks like. I was reassured that we were not alone,
that this fight was larger than the fourteen hunger strikers. Although this
experience was physically challenging, my spirit stayed strong from all the
love and support we received from people all over the city. I was determined
to continue until our victory was attained.

The hunger strike came after years of community pressure demanding
the construction of a second high school to relieve massive overcrowding
at Farragut High School, which was the only high school in Little Village
(La Villita). During the 1998 municipal elections, Mayor Daley held a
press conference in which he promised the construction of three new high
schools, including one for the Little Village community. The press conference was held at the site of a closed-down oil refinery, the present location
of the Little Village/North Lawndale Multiplex. Yet two years later in 2000,
two selective enrollment schools were built (North Side College Prep and
Walter Payton). At the time there was no sight of the school promised for
the Little Village Community. People in the community began to realize
that Mayor Daley's promise was just for the sake of his political campaign,
and he had no intention of keeping that promise.

It was during the spring of 2000 when I joined Tomás Gaete, my
father, a block club organizer for the then–Little Village Development Corporation (LVCDC), that we saw the beginning of the efforts that led to
the hunger strike. After numerous conversations with folks he met while
knocking on doors, the people continuously brought up the question, What
happened to the construction of the high school? the overwhelming concern
parents demonstrated on a daily basis was their children's safety, due to the
large number of students graduating from elementary schools in Little Village who had to travel long distances and across different gang lines in order
to get to high schools in different neighborhood. Parents who sent their
children to Farragut High School felt their children were being subjected to
inhumane learning conditions since the school lacked the adequate space,
calling for the school to turn its closets and hallways into classrooms. The
huge concern demonstrated by community residents informed my father's
decision to focus on educational issues facing our community. Shortly after
my father organized an education committee, when he asked me to join, I
immediately jumped at the chance to work with my teacher, my example to

follow, my hero alongside my older brother Claudio and my younger sister Gema. The education committee worked on collecting petitions, attending Local School Council meetings, and Block Club associations, knocking on doors, marching around the neighborhood, and speaking at Sunday church services to inform residents and gain community support. Our first action was delivering thousands of signatures collected by residents of Little Village in support of building the high school on Thirty-First and Kostner to the board of education, under the leadership Gary Chico, as the president of the board, and Paul Vallas, CEO of Chicago Public Schools (CPS). The petitions were delivered at the board meeting with a serenade by a full Mariachi band, something that had never been done before. We wanted to make sure they heard us loud and clear. However, CPS and Mayor Daley continued to ignore us for about another year and a half, hoping we would go away or get over shadowed by UNO's demand for the construction of a high school at a different location. We knew this was a strategy created to divert attention from the fact that neither Mayor Daley nor Paul Vallas had any intention on investing in the construction of a second community high school. At the time, Daley, Vallas, and Chico were more concerned with "reform" efforts that would soon morph into the policy Renaissance 2010 under the current secretary of Education, Arne Duncan (CEO of CPS during the implementation of the policy).

The decision to stage a hunger strike came after numerous failed attempts to get answers from the Mayor and CPS. Despite resistance from community "stakeholders" (i.e., those who were worried to be in the bad graces of the mayor's office) to engage a hunger strike, we continued to move forward with our plan. The community was organized and ready to fight! Our children were being ignored, disrespected, and subjected to inhumane learning conditions. We had reached our boiling point; the general consensus was that for our children we would sacrifice ourselves. On May 13, 2001, Mother's Day, I, along with thirteen other women and men declared a hunger strike, one that on unbeknownst to any us would last nineteen days. We started as fourteen individuals who after nineteen days of sleeping in tents, weathering heavy rainstorms, meetings with CPS officials, dancing, singing, and sharing our stories transformed into a powerful and tightly woven unit. The hunger strike brought people together in solidarity from across the city, offering their skills, talents, and resources to keep us strong and determined to continue on. Camp Cesar Chavez was transformed into tent city; with every day that passed, more and more people started to come by and offer their help by building stages, cooking us broths, bringing by water, paper, donations, and so much more. At first neighbors just came and left, but slowly people began staying and attending ecumenical services, offered by churches of different denominations participating in daily update, planning meetings, and joining us in protesting the mayor and CPS. Almost two weeks into the hunger strike, during a heated exchange at a board of education meeting with over two hundred supporters in attendance, an irritated Gary Chico revealed that the state capital funds allocated for the construction of the high school in La Villita was used for Walter Payton Magnet School. What! Our nonviolent philosophy had been tested and the room exploded with anger; security guards began to push and shove us out of the meeting room—this time we literally pushed back and defended ourselves. A few days later Gary Chico resigned from his position as board president, followed by Paul Vallas's resignation. Neither admitted that they did not want to be connected to Mayor Daley's shameful actions, but instead reported that their resignations were based on their need to "spend more time with family." A more accurate response would speak to their political aspirations; Chico's for Congress and Vallas for governor. From this moment, the mayor and CPS had to rethink their strategy for moving forward, since their lies had been exposed. I believe these were major factors that led to CPS, committing to the future construction of the high school. Not trusting CPS, we still were not ready to call an end to the hunger strike until we received a definitive timeline for construction. Simultaneously, the same community "stakeholders" that were resistant were now front and center, speaking to the media, setting up back-room deals manipulating the truth, and pushing us to end the strike. A vote was taken by the hunger strikers to end our efforts after nineteen days without food. We called an end to this phase of the fight with the commitment to continue to fight for the construction of the Little Village/Lawndale Multiplex. Thirteen years later and as a parent of a freshman at the Greater Lawndale High School for Social Justice, I can honestly say the fight did not end with its construction, as the school continues to face many challenges.

Tackling the contradictions of community struggle and machine politics in Chicago, the construction of the high school advanced the political and professional career of people who were only marginally involved in the struggle. Meanwhile, many of those who sacrificed their health, and economic well-being, were met with debilitating medical issues, and the loss of employment, including my father who led the organizing efforts to build the school. As I reflect on my experiences of being involved in the struggle against the privatization of public education in Chicago, whether in the forty-three-day occupation of La Casita in Pilsen, or part of the massive mobilizations against school closings, I realize that the sustainability of movements require that those directly impacted have ownership and control over strategies and outcomes. Throughout the process, my biggest lesson was learning the difference between community ownership (direct engagement and personal transformation) and community "buy-in" (compliance with someone else's vision and agenda for our community). The fight was not just for a building or a school, but for our belief that all children deserve a school that respects and honors their humanity as students as well as the community in which it exists. To all who are interested in struggle, don't ever let the notion that something is unwinnable stop you from fighting to achieving it. The only fight we lose is the one we don't fight. *Si se puede! Yes we can!*

Acknowledgments

This book would be impossible to complete without the support of many. Some hold multiple positions in the groups mentioned below, all were instrumental to my process: Ronald and Ada Stovall (my mother and father), Edna Stovall (my grandmother), Angela Odoms Young, Erik Young, and Anita and George Odoms; Tomas Gaete and members of the *huelgistas* who engaged the nineteen-day hunger strike: Manuelita Garcia, Samuel "Sammy" Garcia, Andrea Guzman, Toribio Esteban, Carolina "Caro" Gaete, Gema Gaete, Patricia "Patty" Buenrostro, Claudio Gaete, Linda Zarate, Carolina Perez, Elena Lee, Samuel Garcia, Ruben Magdaleno, Sergio Mojarro, Hugo Seja, and Teresa Yanez; Barbara Love, and Maurianne Adams at the University of Massachusetts Amherst; members of the original and current administration/teaching staff of SOJO: Rito Martinez, Katherine (Katie) Kasper Hogan, Angela Sangha-Gadsen, Ana Herrera, Tracy Van Duinen, Ida Joyce Sia, Phi Pham, Tiffany Ko, Chala Holland, Noelle Jones, Sue Nelson, Cynthia Nambo, Bhumika Gor, Daniel Morales-Doyle, Jackson Potter, Chad Weiden, Linda Becker, David Segura, Tinaya Webb, Lutalo McGee, Brenda Cerda, Angelo "Pepper" Resendez, Emily Alt, Simona Chavez, Matthew Crye, John Reiztel, Yamali Rodriguez, David Hernandez, Xiomara Bustamante, Troy Kamau Laraviere, Jason Flores, Alma Preciado, Linda Boyle, Colleen Lane, Amy Livingston, Omar Marquez, Herman Shelton, Will O'Neil, Melanie Davis, and Kathy Farr; past and current members of the Advisory Local School Council (ALSC): Sandra Mendez, Shirley Jones, Lorena Jasso, Katya Nuques, Cristina Barazza, Bertha Gonzalez, and Jahel Ramirez; members of the original design team: Eric "Rico" Gutstein, Steve Yannias, Brenda Arrendondo, LaShaun Cox, Alicia Serrano, Marisol Damaso, Pat Christopher, Lizandra Linares, and Carol Miller Lieber; members of the Transition Advisory Council (TAC): Carmen Mahon, Tiffany Childress, Jaime DeLeon, Jesus "Chuy" Garcia, Stanley

Merriwether, Joan Caldwell, Josephine "Josie" Yanguas, Linda Corronado, Aquil Charlton, Jorge Roque, Beatrize Santin, Maria Cabral, Sara Villanueva, Fernando Mosqueda, Alyssa Dons, Maria Almazan, Rutilio Martinez, Aurelia Moreno, and Miguel Velazquez; 8th Period 2009: Julio Alvarado, Adriana Alvarez, Angel Arroyo, Silvia Barba, Gloria Campos, George Carr, Mayra Contreras, Rey Dominguez, Joi Elmore, Fanny Garcia, Veronica Gonzalez, Alejandro Hernandez, Darnisha Hill, Antonio Jimenez, Jazmin Johnson, Amy Maldonado, John Mayida, Jose Mejia, Erika Ortiz, Gerardo Pantojas, Alejandra Ramirez, Amparo Ramos, Rut Rodriguez, Victor Rosales, Chloe Robinson, Verenice Valles, and Rocio Villavicencio; those who have served as readers and advisers for the project: Erica Meiners, Connie Wun, Alyssa Garcia, Natalia Delgado, Gabriel Cortez, William Ayers, Michelle Fine, Sumi Cho, Kelly Zen-Yie Tsai, Bree Picower, Richard Benson, Ebony McGee, Michelle Boyd, Fancesca Gaiba, Beth Richie, Lisa "Leigh" Patel-Stevens, Kristen Lynn Buras, Daniel Solorzano, Gloria Ladson-Billings, David Gillborn, Devon Carbado, Richard Delgado, Eric Yamamoto, Cheryl Harris, Kevin Kumashiro, Eric Tang, Tara Betts, Gabrielle "Biba" Fullon, Jeffrey Duncan-Andrade, Patrick Camangian, K. Wayne Yang, Antwi Akom, Allison Tsingtianco-Cubales, Edwin Mayorga, Theadorea "Thea" Berry, Sherick Hughes, Denise Taliaferro-Brasile, and Marvin Lynn; members of (CGCT): Cecily Relucio Huber, Kesh Ross, Kay Fujiyoshi, Ann Aviles, Isaura Pulido, Hosik (Steve) Moon, Terrence (T-Zye) Hamer, and Sonjanita Moore; Isabel Nunez and Members of Chicagoland Researchers and Advocates for Transformative Education; Chicago, New York City, and Oakland coffee shops: Effebina's, Sip Coffeehouse, Sip and Savor Café, Atomix Café, The Bourgeois Pig Café, Sweet Attila's Café, Filter Café, Bridgeport Coffee, Coffee Alley, Café La Catrina, Café Colador, Spazzo Café, Farley's, Au Coquelet, Grand Fare Café, and Grand Lake Coffee. Blessings to the twenty-year squadron: Darius Bright, Dwayne Preston, Gladston "Stone" Sanders, Rahsaan "Rah" Moore, Charles Clemons, Jason "J-Green" Green, Timothy Harper, Creighton Barr, Florence "Phloe" Pontaoe, Joseph "Mark" Salutillo, Suzanne Hollingshead, Dinorah "Dino" Lozano, San Tong, Chauncey B. Ranglin Washington, Vivienne Tan, and Kourtney "Black" Cockrell. May the creator continue to bless Eighty-Seventh Street.

Responsibility to the Word

Into the Work of Putting Our Theories to Practice

There has yet to be an honest national public discussion about race in this country, and there is little hope there will be one soon. This is because it has been much more convenient for those in power to use race as a political football and as a way of sensationalizing issues such as crime than to develop safe public spaces to explore the phenomenon of race down to its deepest dehumanizing emotional roots, which social scientists have to even minutely uncover since it is too painful to do so.

—Stanfield II

Critical Race Theory needs to move. Greater attention to critical coalitions is one area for movement . . . Critical coalitions are real fragile and vibrant. They grow out of strategic community attempts to change the material conditions of people's lives often at great risk to community members. They reflect a refusal to limit coalitions to alliances based solely on short-term common interests or to alliances only among activists and civil-rights lawyers.

—Yamamoto and Su

Yo . . . Meet me on the corner of Thirty-First and Kostner . . . there's gonna be an event there . . .

On May 16, 2001, I received a phone call from my good friend Carolina "Caro" Gaete. She left a message on my voice mail telling me to meet her on the corner of Thirty-First and Kostner. When I finished playing the message,

I vaguely remembered a conversation Caro (Carolina) and I had a couple of weeks back. It was about her and a group of community members banding together to demand quality public education for her neighborhood. Despite only remembering bits and pieces of the story, I drove to the corner of Thirty-First and Kostner, just east of the Thirty-FirstStreet bridge that separated the Chicago neighborhood of Little Village and the southwest suburb of Cicero. Upon getting out of the car, I noticed that there were very few people at the site. Among the various packing factories, semitruck repair shops, a car wash, and a trucking freight drop-off center, there was the barren corner of Thirty-First and Kostner. The site once occupied by a paint factory, had been renamed Camp Cesar Chavez, after the revolutionary champion for farmworkers' rights. Now, on the barren corner stood a network television van with a huge broadcast antenna emerging from the rear bumper, a stage built by the Black Carpenter's association, and a tent stocked with water, chicken stock, and first aid kits.

In addition to myself, there were two or three people looking as dumbfounded as I was. When one of the people walked close to where I was standing, I asked him if he was told to meet at the corner of Thirty-First and Kostner. "Yeah," he replied. "But I don't know where people are." "Me neither," I responded. With that exchange we just laughed and chalked it up to chance that our timing was off. The best I felt I could do at the moment was to sit tight at the site until I saw someone I knew. Caro wasn't answering her phone, so I assumed that she was busy with something. The only problem was that mid-May in Chicago can be freezing. Unfortunately, for me, it was one of those days. Hopefully I would see the group soon. Luckily for me, I looked down the block and noticed a large group of people walking down the middle of Kostner Avenue, as part of a community march. Once the group reached the campsite, a number of community members and public officials gave speeches, while others recited poetry and performed pieces of community political theater. I finally caught up with Caro and she explained that I was witnessing the public declaration of a hunger strike demanding that a high school be built in the community of La Villita (Little Village). Though most of the remarks were in Spanish, I knew from earlier conversations with Caro that the community had planned for a public event to protest Chicago Public Schools (CPS). What I did not know was that this event would come in the form of a hunger strike. This was day three of the strike. The initiative would last nineteen days, where fourteen community members, parents, grandparents, and students went without food, living on chicken broth, water, and juice, demanding that a school be built in their neighborhood.

I knew there had been a struggle in the community of Little Village to get a school. Additionally, I also knew that three selective enrollment magnet schools had been constructed in the city since 1998, but there was nothing in Little Village. Instead of a school that was a neighborhood school, with the only requirements for admission being the completion of eighth grade and that you lived in the neighborhood, Mayor Richard Daley wanted to create the exact opposite. His plan was to create selective enrollment schools, where you had to have a particular test score as an eighth grader to take the entrance exam to be selected for those schools. These schools would serve as his pride and joy, as they served as the anchors to attract affluent families back to the city to buy homes, igniting a gentrification effort that would push poor and working-class African-American and Latino/a families out of the city.

Into the Heart of the Matter

What I did not know, however, was that the community of La Villita was promised a school as part of Daley's 1997 mayoral campaign, one full year before any of the selective enrollment schools were built. To address issues of school overcrowding in one of Chicago's most densely populated neighborhoods, the mayor held a press conference on the corner of Thirty-First and Kostner, promising to build a school. Because, the school in the mayor's original proposal never came to fruition, the community members were protesting the fact that they never got what was promised to them. As a community steeped in community and political activism, they did not take the mayor's actions lying down. Directly connected to the political and educational organizing of the likes of Rudy Lozano and Maria Saucedo (1), community members under the lead of Tomas Gaete, then of the Little Village Community Development Corporation (LVCDC), organized themselves to draw attention to the community's effort to ensure that a high school was built for their community. Common to education organizing in Chicago, the force behind educational justice is largely motivated by community-driven initiatives. Noted in the works of Danns (2004), Lipman (2010), and Hare (2007), Chicago possesses a robust history of communities organizing for educational justice. Deeply connected to the political economy of the city, community members and community-based organizations must develop explicit knowledge of the function of the city. If they do not, they run the risk of succumbing to the whims of CPS and the mayor's office, who rarely operate for the interests of low-income communities of color.

The Need for Counterstory

Referenced as "the Word" by Charles Laurence III, our stories, specifically in relation to racism and hegemony, are "subjective, consciously historical, and revisionist" (Laurence III in Crenshaw et al., 1995, p. 337). Where some may consider Laurence's statements as conflicting, critical race theory (CRT) locates the stories of people of color in the United States and the larger world as historically relevant and valid. Understood as "counterstory," I agree with Laurence that our stories (in conjunction with the historical record) are key to "praxis . . . in the ongoing work of the scholar as teacher (and activist)" (ibid.). Through our subjectivity we are able to acknowledge and validate the myriad experiences and perspectives. Ours is not the only viewpoint, but a perspective that is often excluded. Due to these omissions, it is critical for the activist/scholar to intentionally engage the political exercise of claiming space to tell our story. The following pages, in the spirit of Laurence's words, are an attempt to grapple with a complex collection of counterstories with numerous moving parts while theorizing in the first person.

As part of a larger "counternarrative," this book "seek(s) to document the persistence of racism from the perspectives of those injured and victimized by its legacy" (Yosso 2006, 60). By engaging in counternarrative, the remainder of this document is an account of an attempt to carefully and critically test the theoretical construct of CRT and its utility as critical community praxis. Through the advent of counternarrative, my involvement on the design team for the Greater Lawndale High School for Social Justice (SOJO) operated under the premise of a commitment to challenge White supremacy/racism by working with community members focused on gaining access to quality education. Discussed in detail throughout the ensuing chapters, counterstory highlights the multiple contradictions between myself and community members when things do not go as planned, delving into the messiness of disagreements rooted in competing visions for the school, the adjacent neighborhoods, and beyond. The hope is to challenge the traditional colonial relationship between university "partners" and community members and the ability of university-based researchers to support community-based initiatives once a substantial victory is achieved (in this case the building of the school).

Critical Race Theory and Critical Race Praxis:
Putting Theory to Work

As a succinct, operative, working definition, Black studies scholar, Manning Marable's definition of racism is of particular salience to this book.

Racism as "a system of ignorance, exploitation, and power used to oppress African-Americans, Latino/as, Asians (South, East, and Middle East), Pacific Americans, American Indians and other people on the basis of ethnicity, culture, mannerisms, and color" (Marable 1996, 170). Paring a class analysis of the construct, Vaught provides a layered account of racism and how it is intertwined with class and other categorical divisions.

> Racism is a ubiquitous, highly structured socioeconomic dynamic shaped largely by the cultural and material economy of property. Material resources are inequitably distributed through the reigning dominion of rights. . . . racism is participation in an ideologic system of rights that maintains the dominance of Whiteness across all facets of the socioeconomic order. (Vaught 2011, 42)

Additionally, I couple the Marable and Vaught definitions of racism with a working definition of White supremacy. Instead of thinking of the concept as a description of the practices of organizations that have as their direct goal to engage in acts of violence against people of color and other marginalized communities, White supremacy is the ideological concept that holds the media-influenced and government-supported mainstream values of American White, Western European–descended heterosexual, Protestant, Christian males as normative. John Stanfield II's understanding of race as "a complex human experience of multiple identities with a vast range of heterogeneous cultural experiences both conscious and unconscious, within, outside and across racialized categorical boxes" is key to explicating the conundrum of a concept categorically ignored for its systemic function (Stanfield II in Zuberi and Bonia-Silva 2008, 277–278). Despite the sentiment of a "postracial" moment with the 2008 election of Barack Obama as the forty-fourth president of the United States, America is not in the postracial Valhalla it purports itself to be to the rest of the world. Cloaked in the rhetoric of "American values," beneath the surface lies an ideology of hyperindividualistic, self-indulgent, neoliberal, free-market rationales that justify the exclusion of particular groups from resources necessary in creating thriving schools and communities. If it is not a complete exclusion, then it is a prescribed, limited admission to said schools that in many cases reifies the original intent of exclusion. In Chicago, this often results in the targeting of low-income/working-class African-American and Latino/a families by charter schools as more viable options than neighborhood public schools.

For many people of color in the United States, racism remains salient and real. Coupled with economic/wealth disparity, gender discrimination, patriarchy, heteronormativity, ageism, and ableism, racism should be understood as complex, intricate, and perpetually shifting. Vaught is correct in that "the deeper logic is Black (and Brown) children do not *happen* to be poor, but are *necessarily* poor" (Vaught, 50). The "necessity" of their poverty comes by way of an ideological pairing of poverty and race that is fueled and reinforced through a belief that to be a poor person of color is in concert with the natural order of things.

From my point of view, one of the more salient examples comes by way of Michelle Alexander's book *The New Jim Crow* (2010). In stating that there are more African-Americans currently incarcerated than there were listed as slaves in 1850, we are compelled to understand that disparity has not ended in the United States, but has instead shifted to systems of mass incarceration mirroring the days of manumitted servitude (Alexander 2010, cite). Additionally, the cities of Philadelphia and Chicago have collectively closed or repurposed nearly two hundred schools over the last fifteen years, further marginalizing and disenfranchising scores of low-income/working-class African-American and Latino/a communities (CEJE 2014). The current political moment in public education coupled with the dominant rationale for a deepening carceral state is reflective of the shifting nature of racism. Instead of an explicit process located in acts of individual bigotry, racism/White supremacy stands as a complex, amorphous, shifting, sometimes overt, often covert manifestation of an insidious system imbued in human subjugation. As the set of layered and complex iterations between people and systems, racism/White supremacy deserves our undivided attention.

For the remainder of this book, racism is paired with other forms of oppression, most notably class, to understand the layers of my participation as a member of SOJO's design team. I agree with Leonardo (2009) in that the positioned conflict between race and class is shortsighted and should be understood as a paired phenomenon in which one element is rarely present without the other (Leonardo 2009, 45). In historical and contemporary pairings, the salience of racism/White supremacy has been downplayed and often subsumed with class as the overriding analytical frame by which to explain inequality, exploitation, and alienation. In the instance of my participation on the design team, racism/White Supremacy exists in ideological and systemic forms when identifying the relationship between low-income/working-class communities of color and school systems. Chicago, in all of its perpetually shifting policies and facades of "development," provides a prima facie example of the aforementioned relationship.

In the same vein, theoretical understandings were not my first concern when I was approached to become a member of the design team. Instead, after numerous interactions, observations, and reflections with the design team and community members, the tenets of critical race theory became apparent as the theoretical construct that best spoke to the purpose and direction of our exploits. In my previous interactions with CRT, I have been outspoken about my distaste for theories that claim to be aimed at social justice, while offering few connections to community engagement and authentic accountability of researchers to communities we work with. For this book I use a composite of the tenets developed by the likes of Ladson-Billings and Tate (1995) and Solorzano in education (1997), while incorporating Yamamoto (1997) and Bell (1997) in legal theory. Coupled with the recent advances of the construct by Lynn and Dixson (2013), Carter-Andrews and Tuitt (2013), and Vaught (2011), the constellation of theoretical underpinnings guide my framing of the experience as a member of the design team.

Although CRT has its grounding in legal theory, it has been adopted by scholars in education to address issues faced by urban youth of color in schools. From legal scholarship, I use the construct of interest convergence and critical race praxis. Coined by Derrick Bell in the 1980s, interest convergence is the idea that mainstream (read White) systems of power will only move toward racial justice to the extent that it will jointly advance the interests of mainstream society. As Bell uses the Cold War example of the US government attempting to appeal to the good graces of the noncommunist developed world through the *Brown v. Board* decision, we find a similar interest with the development of SOJO. In the case of Chicago Public Schools, CEO Paul Vallas's transition from CEO of CPS to an electoral run for governor created a conundrum. As the administration of newly appointed CEO Arne Duncan did not want to begin its tenure by thwarting the demands of hunger strikers calling for quality education, Instead they made the decision to build the school (cite Bell).

Critical race theory, as a theoretical construct in education, "seeks to inform theory, research, pedagogy, curriculum and policy" (Solozano and Yosso in Yosso 2006). Operating on theoretical and practical level, CRT in education should be included as making a contribution to praxis, in that it supports the necessary actions of communities engaging the day-to-day realities of demanding quality education. Education, as the process of making informed decisions to improve the human condition through critical analysis and action, is not confined to the walls of a school building. Instead, it can also operate as the political exercise intent on providing communities that experience disinvestment, marginalization, and isolation with the ability to analyze and change their conditions. Inherent to this process is working with people and groups in communities to develop the capacity to utilize their own skills and expertise to address issues and concerns that threaten their existence.

Continuing the contributions from legal theory, I seek to incorporate Yamamoto's concept of critical race praxis. Through this construct he calls for those who are concerned with justice while being employed in academia to spend less time with "abstract theorizing" and more time on the ground with communities and groups who are demanding justice around issues that affect people's daily lives (e.g., education, employment, health care, gender injustice, environmental rights, LGBTQA concerns, etc.). The idea is not to position those employed in academia as "saviors," but to develop solidarity through the process of working *with* others instead of doing research *on* them.

Simultaneously, this book utilizes CRT tenets developed in education scholarship. As key theoretical constructs in framing the story of SOJO's design team, the Solorzano and Yosso tenets of CRT operate as one of the foundational underpinnings of the book. Whereas the italicized quotes are directly from Solorzano and Yosso, the responding sentences are how I use the tenets to frame my involvement at SOJO.

> *The intercentricity of race and racism:* Race and racism are not monolithic concepts. Instead, they are complex, dynamic, and malleable social constructions endemic to life in the United States. Due to their shifting contexts, definitions of race can include and exclude groups depending on the historical moment. For example, whereas immigrating and native-born Latinos/as in the United States were once categorized as "White," they have now been falsely vilified as the culprits responsible for taking jobs from US citizens. By recognizing the historical and social evolutions of race, CRT seeks to problematize the paradigm.

> *Challenge to dominant ideology:* The master narrative on African-American and Latino/a students in public education is engulfed in theories of deficit. CRT challenges the master narrative on the inability of students of color to excel in academic settings.

> *Commitment to social justice:* CRT offers itself as a theoretical and methodological paradigm aimed at the elimination of race, class, and gender oppression.

Centrality of experiential knowledge: The knowledge of people of color in the fight against hegemonic forces in education is legitimate, valid, and necessary in creating spaces for said communities to engage justice work.

Transdisciplinary perspective: CRT borrows from legal theory, ethnic studies, women's studies, sociology, history, philosophy, economics, and other fields to argue for a comprehensive analysis of the functions of race and racism in education. (Solorzano and Yosso 2002, 7–8)

Initially CRT in education calls for the ability to analyze policy with a race-conscious lens. In this process it can offer critical questions around the formation of policies that directly affect communities of color. As insurgent scholarship rooted in critique and action, CRT "seeks to inform theory, research, pedagogy, curriculum, and policy" (Solozano and Yosso in Yosso 2006). Operating on theoretical and practical level, CRT in education has the potential to contribution to praxis, in that it supports "action and reflection in the world in order to change it" (Freire 1973). I understand CRT as central to the larger political project and strategy that helps to frame my experience as a researcher, concerned citizen, and member of the design team in the creation of SOJO. Because the story of the design team is often complex, messy, entangled, and dense, framing the story as an act of praxis is reflective of the necessary checks and balances of praxis-centered work needed within coalitions to maintain accountability to justice-based initiatives.

For these reasons, research with students and families in school and community spaces are important to engage from the perspective of co-constructor or co-collaborator. Doing so challenges CRT scholars to work at the intersection of multiple theoretical and methodological approaches that coalesce in our work on the ground in/with communities (Lynn and Parker 2002; Lynn and Jennings 2006; Fine and Cammarota 2008, Meiners and Ibanez-Carrasco 2004; Tuhiwai-Smith 2012). By interrupting the traditional research paradigm suggesting "objectivity" or "validity," CRT, like engaged scholarship, youth participatory action research (YPAR), critical ethnography, and community-based participatory research before it encourages scholars to get "close" to our work. Encapsulated in this approach is the understanding that any work toward the larger justice project in education will sometimes require making tough, uncomfortable decisions that often have the potential to isolate scholars from the groups they work with

(Tuhiwai-Smith 2012). As Yamamoto has offered a working definition of Critical Race Praxis (CRP) in legal scholarship, my attempt is to utilize the constellation of legal, educational tenets of CRT. From critical race praxis in legal studies I incorporate the tenets of Yamamoto's working definition of race praxis from *Interracial Justice*.

- ***Conceptual:*** Examining the racialization of a controversy and the interconnecting influences of heterosexism, patriarchy, and class while locating that examination in a critique of the political economy (Yamamoto 1999, 130).

- ***Performative:*** Answering the question as to what practical steps are responsive to the specific claim and who should act on that claim (131).

- ***Material:*** Inquiring into changes, both socio-structural and the remaking of the democratic structure of public institutions, in the material conditions of racial oppression. Examples would include access to fair housing, health care, quality education, employment, and so on (132).

- ***Reflexive:*** Commitment to the continual rebuilding of theory in light of the practical experiences of racial groups engaged in particular antiracist struggles (ibid).

From both sets of tenets, this book discusses how they operate on the ground in the attempt to remain responsible to a community-driven initiative.

In doing so, the goal of my work is not to provide an "objective" lens. Instead, I utilize the writings of Charles Laurence III, in that our stories, by nature of the subject matter (in this case, racism, and hegemony) are "subjective, consciously historical, and revisionist" (Laurence III in Crenshaw et al. 1995, 337). Where some may consider Professor Laurence's statements to be conflicting with traditional research paradigms, CRT locates the stories of people of color in the United States and the larger world as historically relevant and valid. I agree with Laurence that our stories (in conjunction with the historical record) are key to "praxis . . . in the ongoing work of the scholar as teacher (and activist)" (ibid.). Through our subjectivity, we are able to acknowledge and validate the myriad experiences and perspectives. Ours is not the only viewpoint, but a perspective that is often excluded; because of these omissions, it is critical for the scholar/activist to intentionally engage the political exercise of claiming space to tell our story.

Through "counternarrative," the proceeding pages "seek to document the persistence of racism from the perspectives of those injured and victimized by its legacy (Yosso 2006, 60). Enforcing the concept of counternarrative, my involvement on the SOJO design team operates in solidarity with a community's commitment to challenge white supremacy/racism by gaining access to quality education. Narrative, as a conduit by which to communicate issues and concerns, encourages us to engage practical means by which to address issues brought forward by racism. As scholarship committed to larger justice project in education, the responsibility becomes to move beyond our rhetoric and push toward developing models of praxis. With this in mind, the remainder of the book seeks to explore, grapple with, and reflect on the following three impressions:

- The utilization of CRT and CRP to inform the process of creating an urban high school across political, social, economic, and racial boundaries.

- The responsibility of critical race scholars in education to community-driven efforts.

- Critical analysis of the tacit and explicit challenges, tensions, moments of clarity, and small victories imbued in the process of community members, students, teachers, families, and researchers in negotiating tensions between hegemonic educational systems and community self-determination to create an urban high school.

Yamamoto encourages scholars to pay specific "attention to theory translation and frontline action" (Yamamoto 1999, 129). Where his initial suggestions were directed toward attorneys and law professors, I incorporate his suggestions that entail the work of educational researchers who are concerned with educational and racial justice.

In addition to the aforementioned impressions, one question the book grapples with is: How can CRT make real its connection to the material conditions of people's lives? (Yamamoto and Su 2006, 390–1). As part of his method, Yamamoto suggests that race praxis is characterized by reflective action (ibid.). Such reflection is based on the application of theoretical concepts to the work done in solidarity with communities, and the recasting of said concepts in relation to our on-the-ground experiences. In my work on the design team, this entails reflection on the "nuts and bolts" work, which includes developing the proposal for the school, interviewing prospective teachers, and presenting in community forums, while casting the process through a CRT lens. Taking this into account, I frame communication between myself, members of the design team, community organizations, CPS, and the respective Latino/a and African-American communities of Little Village and North Lawndale as work within the nexus of engaged community scholarship and CRT.

Toward a Politics of Interruption

I am using "politics of interruption" to describe the ways in which community members from La Villita and North Lawndale actively resist and navigate local and state power in demanding quality education. In the case of SOJO, the dynamic operates on two specific levels. First is at the hegemonic level of CPS—despite the fact that many people of color are employed by a central office, it has not impeded its function to maintain the status quo of racist, neoliberal policies that continue to limit the educational opportunities for low-income African-American and Latino/a residents of the city. The second level identifies the multilayered power relations in a hypersegregated city. Chicago is a city where the political machine and geographic boundaries create an instance where many neighborhoods populated by people of color have little contact with each other, interracially. Unless they are in proximity or adjacent to each other, the city's history of segregation has created an instance where some residents rarely venture beyond their neighborhood's boundaries. As North Lawndale is the neighborhood chosen by CPS to address its compliance with a standing consent decree to desegregate, the inclusion of African-American residents in a school located in the predominantly Latino/a neighborhood of Little Village (La Villita) was not a transparent or seamless process. Despite the neighborhoods being adjacent to each other, it becomes a challenging task to create a situation between two groups that do not have frequent, conflict-free interactions with each other. Both levels of understandings represent difficult, but necessary conversations that need to happen regarding race.

Physical and geographical challenges notwithstanding, the struggle of community members from North Lawndale and La Villita to engage each other in the process of creating a high school still stands as "interruption" to the status quo of substandard education for low-income communities of color. In addition to the monumental success of seeing the school come to fruition, it should also be understood as a flawed attempt to engage the African-American community of North Lawndale. Despite the goodwill efforts of those who genuinely welcomed the idea of including African-American youth, their inclusion introduced tensions to the process. Hypersegregation makes it difficult to engage meaningful, intentional partnerships. Coupled with the political machine often pitting communities against each other in the struggle for reportedly scarce resources, the struggle for quality schools can be a minefield if you're not paying attention. Still in fact, the interruption is an important one in that it represents the efforts to create a socially and racially shared school community.

A Note on Social Justice: Against the Rhetoric of Popular "Activist-Speak"

Over the last decade, I have become concerned when I see the term *social justice* in relationship to almost anything that appears nonconforming to the mainstream status quo. Similar to earlier buzzwords like *multicultural education* or *critical pedagogy*, which have their genesis in radical possibilities, both have been largely reduced to "school-speak," to be used as progressive academic banter. Even though organizations like the National Council for Accreditation of Teacher Education (NCATE) removed the term *social justice* from its accreditation standards in 2009; the term in other instances has joined the ranks of "popular-speak" in certain education/activist circles. Personally, I continue to struggle with how the term is perceived in my understandings of the construct. Expressed in earlier writings (Ayers, Quinn, & Stovall 2009, Stovall & Morales-Doyle in Hobbel & Chapman, 2010), social justice continues to operate as a goal to work toward, instead of an explicit singular measure determined by a particular set of actions.

For myriad reasons, this brings about a set of contradictions in the attempt to articulate my experience as a member of the design team and beyond. Where I am reluctant to make a claim that the work I engage is an example of social justice, I also want to articulate explicit solidarity with those who engage and struggle with the concept and continue to use "social justice" in the title and work of their respective organizations/collectives. I agree with community and youth organizers that "justice," in its most grounded sense, is best determined by those who have experienced the actions that impede quality of life and access to resources that contribute to a thriving existence (injustice). Those outside of the initial struggle may have the ability to contribute to the expressed condition of victory for the group experiencing the injustice, but they cannot hijack and subsequently control the processes initiated by people at the grassroots/community level.

Although common in many university/community partnerships, the following pages document a process that seeks to interrupt said paradigm.

Simultaneously, *social justice* as terminology, ideology, and praxis should be interrogated in perpetuity. Although it has been compromised to some degree (as many things are), my concern is that the term maintains its ties to a radical imaginary. At best, I can offer a working definition of what the term envelops in this account. As a practice that seeks to contribute to the larger project of social justice in education, this book considers social justice in education to be part of an *individual contribution to the collective efforts to articulate the day-to-day processes and actions utilized in communities and classrooms centered in critical analysis and reflection for the purpose of changing our conditions.* Because it is by no stretch of the imagination an absolute, my attempt to work with others to support the larger project of social justice in education is indicative of a personal and collective struggle. These processes include the critical examination of power as it relates to race, class, gender, age, sexual orientation, and disability coupled with action plans and concrete strategies. While this document does not seek to offer the definitive example of social justice in education, it is, however, an attempt to politically, socially, and pedagogically ground my work moving forward.

In and Out of the Contradictions— Some Notes on Where I Enter

For myself, the hunger strike serves as a necessary interruption to the status quo of substandard education for low-income/working-class Black and Latino/a students in Chicago. Historically this has amounted to CPS imposing new "innovations" on communities, ignoring the manufactured inequitable conditions that have shaped the educational experience of the aforementioned. By interrupting the status quo, community members of Little Village and later North Lawndale challenged CPS to remain accountable to the communities they are supposed to serve. When I was informed about the strike by one of the *huelgistas* (hunger strikers), it reminded me of some of the tenets of community organizing in terms of speaking truth to power, remaining accountable to the groups you work in solidarity with, and meeting people where they're at, to ground the work in a mutual appreciation for the skills and dispositions that everyone brings to the table. These practices were key throughout the trials and errors of the design team, as I was brought into the process by one of the *huelgistas*, first as an observer of the hunger strike and then as members of the curriculum committee that met in Caro's house to ponder questions about curriculum, social justice, and the current political economy. Following a yearlong hiatus after our meeting, I was brought back to a community discussion about forming an oversight board for the development of the Little Village Multiplex. For these reasons, and throughout this book, I operate on numerous fronts; first as a concerned citizen, second as a member of the design team, and third as researcher/documentarian responsible for struggling with, recording, and reflecting on the process of creating SOJO, currently housed in the Lawndale/Little Village Multiplex.

Understanding the permanent, engrained, and enduring properties of racism posed many challenges for the design team. Because Chicago is a hypersegregated city, the communities of Little Village and North Lawndale, despite their geographic adjacent relationship, have little contact with each other. Despite brief moments in political campaigns and community organizing, African-American (Black) and Latino/a residents were forced to educate themselves about each other. Though some members in both groups were reluctant at first, others took the issue head-on. They reminded the group of the collective struggle of Black and Latino/a peoples and how racism/White supremacy has functioned in the past to divide and conquer, resulting in distrust and self-segregation; coupled with the historical legacy of CPS and its treatment of Black and Latino/a youths traditionally labeled as low income, as members of the design team we continually found ourselves at a crossroads when it came between choosing accountability to the initial community-driven initiative and compliance with CPS policy. It became especially difficult when the people responsible for communicating CPS policy and mandates to the design team in many cases were African-American and Latino/a. Even more troubling was the fact that many understood how hegemonic bureaucracies derail community initiatives. On numerous occasions we were "advised" on how not to "ruffle the feathers" of CPS in creating the high school. In the liberal sense, they felt that they were "doing us a favor." In reality, it often felt like they were agents of the state with the sole intent of making sure the high school would never see the light of day.

Responsibility to this story means that I must contend with a process fraught with contradictions and intricacies. Because I am deeply ingrained in the inconsistencies and complexity, I am implicated in my attempt to articulate a complex story with many moving parts and interpretations. In many instances, my account to people familiar with the struggle will read as jagged and uneven. Yet to others, it may appear too congratulatory and centered in community victories. Within these contradictions, the challenge of putting theory to practice is a considerable, but necessary task in the hope of remaining accountable to community members, community organizations, teachers, students, and administrators as the high school moves forward. Embracing these contradictions, I understand my work as raising

> "Intensely personal questions about ourselves—as raced, gendered, and classed actors—and where we fit into the relations of power, of domination and subordination, in our societies."
> (Apple in Gitlin 1994, x)

As an African-American male teacher/researcher/university professor with a background in youth work and community organizing with limited Spanish language ability, I am closely acquainted with the relations of power between municipal bodies (in this case an urban public school system), community organizations, and community residents. Operating as a lifelong Chicagoan, I have worked with numerous community organizations, classroom teachers, and other school-based groups on developing concepts of justice-centered education. All are deeply intentional political acts, with the purpose of interrupting systems of power traditionally used to marginalize and isolate low-income/working-class communities of color.

At the same time, I am neither a resident of Little Village nor of North Lawndale. Because I was called into the design team process as an education "expert," in many ways I feel as if I operate as an insider/outsider (Windance Twine, 2000). I am "inside" the process in that I was a member of the design team and continue to work with students, teachers, and families at SOJO. For the reasons beginning this paragraph, I would still be considered "outside" of the process. The documentation of my interactions is similar to Tang's application of Gloria Anzaldua's concept of "las Nepanterlas." This is a person that moves "within and between different institutional structures, different disciplines, different cultures and different publics and using this movement to 'facilitate passage between multiple worlds' to create more inclusive, culturally responsive, and academically relevant learning communities" (Tang in Cole 2009, 239). Furthering this concept, I also team-teach a course at SOJO with one of my former undergraduate students. An additional two of my former undergraduate students are on SOJOs teaching staff. Compounding my involvement, I serve as a member of the Advisory Local School Council (ALSC), with recommendation power for budget oversight and the hiring and removal of principals.

Within these responsibilities, I am regularly navigating the responsibility of researcher, documentarian, volunteer teacher, arbiter, and communicator. In light of the aforementioned responsibilities, I am not operating from an "objective" stance. Instead, because I am deeply engrained in the process, I must engage my contradictions and "closeness" to the work.

Simultaneously, I am outside of the process due to my nonresidence in either community, coupled with my limited Spanish-speaking ability. Further solidifying my outsider status would be my employment as a tenured professor at an urban land-grant institution. Compounding the dynamic is the fact that this university has a tumultuous history with some local communities, resulting in mass displacement and gentrification in the name of "development." Instead of bypassing these contradictions, I enter these conflicting realities to highlight the myriad embodied contradictions in my struggles throughout the design team process and beyond.

Heeding the challenge of Linda Tuhiwai Smith, in recognizing the historical colonial relationship between communities and universities, I enter the process understanding that my work would be impossible without the community's blessing. I agree that "it is not ethical to walk away, or simply to carry out projects which describe what is already known" (Tuhiwai Smith 2012, 140). In this sense the roles and relationships go beyond the ethics of traditional qualitative research and demand transparency of my intentions with the people I work with who are not representatives of the university.

For these reasons I believe my work, along with the work of others, should be "reconceptualized so that it can more powerfully act on some of the most persistent and important problems of our schools, namely those surrounding issues of race, class, and gender" (Gitlin 1994, ix). Education, as a process of making informed decisions to improve the human condition through critical analysis, reflection, and action, is not confined to the walls of a school building. Instead, it should simultaneously be considered a political exercise with the intent of working in solidarity with historically marginalized and isolated communities to analyze and change systems of power. For these reasons, this work cannot take place without a comprehensive, working knowledge of the functions of race and racism and its effect on our daily lives. As scholarship, the hope is that it continues to challenge the status quo while engaging the contradictions of embedded work in the aftermath of a major community victory. In stepping away from the boundaries of objectivity and into the realm of real life, our "researcher stance" should be challenged, interrogated, and reframed.

Method and Mistakes: Struggle and Accountability
in Community Contexts

Without lamenting or engaging in an unnecessarily long diatribe about my struggles as a graduate student, I can say that I continue to worry as to whether or not I will retain the ability to make my research accessible to the people I work with outside of the academy. Many times the struggle in reading piles of manuscripts, policy papers, and journal articles is to avoid the tragic mistake of adopting "highbrow" language that only makes sense to other academics. As irritating as this was as a graduate student, it becomes almost unbearable as a university professor. While I claim my position in the universe of academics who actively refuse to let the academy define their humanity, I take this position understanding the inherent con- tradictions. Despite my distaste, I remain employed in a relatively secure, tenure-track position at a university. As an occupation laden with privilege, it is often much safer for me to articulate positions that go against the grain of mainstream K–12 educational trends. With a fickle economy and fewer opportunities for people to acquire high-quality jobs that offer a living wage, tenure-track employment academia is significantly distanced from a person making minimum wage with child-rearing responsibilities.

In light of the aforementioned, the process I engage to ensure modi- cums of accuracy and responsibility is one that borrows from a bevy of traditions. As of late I am extremely impressed with the work of Ginwright (2010) in his manuscript on Black youth and radical healing. Presenting a process that incorporates the improvisational nature of jazz, he incorporates a broad constellation of strategies to capture the depth and breadth of his project. Pairing jazz and methodology as the constructs by which to "move beyond simplistic explanations, descriptions and predictions," his work effortlessly maneuvers musical and textual examples to explain his method of accountability to the youth workers and young people he has encoun- tered in his time with the organization Leadership Excellence (Ginwright 2010, 20). His process offers critical guideposts for my own research that seeks to "inform and inspire . . . pose new questions, challenge assumptions and move together in an entirely different direction" (21). Where my own work may not reach the proscribed goals, I move forward in my process humbly and cautiously.

As the amalgamation of my experiences, processes, and reflections as a member of SOJOs design team, this book is not reflective of the tradi- tional longitudinal study or extended case study. However, there are elements that are consistent within both methodologies in that the processes and reflections occur over a thirteen-year period (2001–2014) with a relatively consistent group of people in the same setting. Many of these people were responsible for reading chapters while in draft form, offering suggestions and corrections, ensuring accuracy to the document. As my own methods of member-checking and triangulation, the process of creating this account was developmental in that a broad collection of participants contributed to this book.

Beginning with my initial observations of the strike to my team-teaching a class at SOJO, there are significant gaps over the aforementioned time period. Simultaneously, this account is the collection of field notes (from design team meetings, classrooms, main offices of community organizations, community settings, homes of teachers, community residents, design team members, etc.), interviews, informal conversations, archival research to assemble a puzzle of complex, shifting, sometimes conflicting pieces that don't necessarily "fit" as nicely as the pieces of a store-bought puzzle. Nevertheless, I was not in the position of the passive observer and was immersed in the process, including extensive conversations with other design team members, teachers, students, public officials, CPS representatives, community organizers, and community residents, all of which were integral to the process. In the spirit of Ginwright's jazz-influenced approach to methodology, my struggle to create a coherent document is rooted in observation, description, history, and action (Ginwright, 21).

Scope and Limitations

In recognition of the spirit and commitment of the *huelgistas*, the following pages are limited to my experiences in particular set of moments in the larger community struggle to develop the high school. Whereas there are three other schools housed in the Little Village Lawndale Multiplex (Multicultural Academy of Scholarship, World Languages, Infinity Math, and Science Academy), the focus of this document is the process that shepherds SOJO into fruition. Each school secured their own design team as part of the effort to start the schools simultaneously in the Fall of 2005. Similar to this account, I'm confident their process also includes the myriad complexities in developing a school from the ground up. In the same vein, there were design-team meetings in the earlier stages of the process that were held collectively, but each school was responsible for submitting its own proposal to CPS. The majority of this book highlights the times when we were required to separate into our respective groups and develop the proposal for SOJO. Chapter 2 explains more of the collective processes of the four design teams and the TAC, whereas the remainder of the book is focused in the story of SOJO's formation.

The document is chronological in terms of the chapters, but is not the comprehensive account of the hunger strike and the subsequent time between the schools' approval and the beginning of the formation of the Transition Advisory Council (TAC) and design teams. Because some events took place simultaneously, it is a difficult task at times to articulate the layers of events happening at the same time. Additionally, although the hunger strike was integral to my work on the design team, the majority of the document is dedicated to the work I participated in after the hunger strike. To provide some context for my participation, chapter 1 offers a discussion of the hunger strike and the subsequent events leading to my participation on the design team. As always, my participation in the process would not have been possible if not for the efforts of members in the neighborhoods of Little Village and North Lawndale in organizing for quality education.

Additionally, due to the shifts and changes in the CPS and the City of Chicago, the book is laden with acronyms. A glossary has been provided to guide readers through the maze of acronyms used in the CPS, along with changes and shifts in local, state, and federal education policy. The idea is not to succumb to policy jargon, but accuracy in documenting the story requires the inclusion of said acronyms to provide proper context. The story of the SOJO design team takes place in a particular political economy that includes seismic shifts in the ways schools are perceived and organized in urban areas. SOJOs design team, existing in said tensions, provides an example of community resistance to neoliberal education policy, often resulting in further marginalization of communities of color.

In remaining responsible to those who have or have not provided me with permission to use their names, I will alert readers where it is the person's "real name" or a pseudonym. Because many of those interviewed are still employed in CPS, it is important to respect their wishes of confidentiality. Even though it is illegal for CPS to engage in any sort of repercussion, it is extremely difficult to hold them accountable in a politically charged city like Chicago.

In addition to the usual uses of italics, I have also taken the liberty to use italics for two distinct purposes. The first is to highlight significance of the italicized work or phrase to my relationship to the SOJO design team. Second, in my attempt to tell the story from a CRT perspective, some of the introductory stories in chapters are italicized to give readers a sense of how the counterstory operates. I also want to mention that I use

African-American and "Black" and Latino/a and "Brown" interchangeably. Black and Brown, though contested in some places, represent a collective understanding of how many residents still see themselves in their respective communities.

Overview of Chapters

Chapter 1 describes the communities of Little Village and North Lawndale. Specifically, it speaks to hidden tensions between both communities as a desegregation mandate ordered that the school contain students from North Lawndale, a historical African-American community adjacent to Little Village. The hunger strike serves as the catalyst to excavate the tensions that arose during the design team process within the community of Little Village and between Little Village and North Lawndale residents. Chapter 1 returns to the concept of CRT and applies it to the events following the hunger strike and the formation of the design team. It explores the tenets of CRT in relationship to education and the authors' work on the design team. Chapter 2 outlines the process that created the design teams. Chapter 3 analyzes the role of experiential knowledge in community-based educational initiatives. A series of counterstories speak to the tensions among all of the groups (researchers, community members, community organizers, CPS, CPS partners, etc.) regarding issues of race, class, ethnicity, power, and educational policy. Beginning with the original committees given the charge to make recommendations for the design, curriculum, and governance of the high school, chapter 4 takes the readers into the initial conversations with Chicago Public Schools and its various partners. Chapter 4 challenges critical race theorists to make tangible connections to the material conditions of the lives of the communities in which we work. By highlighting the process of school development, this chapter speaks to the "nuts and bolts" of preparing a school for its opening day. Chapter 5 documents the attempt to bring the original promise of the design team to fruition. Using Gloria Ladson-Billings concept of "educational debt," the chapter seeks to reframe common notions of the "achievement gap." By understanding the current situation with youth of color in urban classrooms as one of a "debt" that is owed to said students, due to years of disinvestment and marginalization, the chapter speaks to the classroom as the site for critical race praxis. Chapter 6 returns to the questions posed in chapter 1 and documents my reflections in relationship to CRT as community praxis. It acknowledges that the process of community engagement can be uneven, complicated, and trying. Chapter 7 recalls the first eight weeks of the 2012–2013 school year, where CPS engaged in a frontal attack to destabilize the school. Couched under the guise of a "personnel decision," the chapter documents the resolve of the community to restabilize the school.

The pages that follow comprise my attempts to articulate an example of researcher responsibility to community-driven efforts. From the outset, I remain hopeful that the tattered layers of my attempt to document my involvement reads as a humble account of my mistakes, missteps, and stumbles toward justice.

Chapter 1

Hunger Strike

History, Community Struggle, and Political Gamesmanship

September 6, 2005

Like most first days of school in Chicago, it was a hot day after the Labor Day holiday. Spirits were high as students descended on the brand-new campus, ready to go to class for the first time in a brand-new, $73-million-dollar building equipped with an Olympic-sized swimming pool, two professional quality gymnasiums, computer corridors, and a collegiate-style library with bay windows and artistic steel structures adorning the entrance. Using the service entrance to enter the building, I was amazed that the structure was finally finished, with all the politics that go into the development of new schools in Chicago. Even though minor construction was still taking place as students were entering the building, the structure itself was testament to something much deeper—a process whereby lives were placed in harm's way for an equitable education for students in the neighborhoods of Little Village and North Lawndale.

I was surprised as I approached the building to see a couple of the former hunger strikers holding placards and signs. At the original planning of the opening of the high school, there was supposed to be a grandiose ceremony, attended by the mayor of the city and the CEO of Chicago Public Schools. Because they decided to attend an event at another school in the city, the first day at the building was without the fanfare of many "dog-and-pony" photo opportunities public officials are known for when anything is considered "new" or "innovative." Nevertheless, there stood the community activists/residents holding the signs and passing out pamphlets. Because I had a meeting with a teacher, I wasn't able to read the signs or pamphlets. As the school day continued, I checked to see if the community residents were still around after the first period of classes.

It's always interesting how the rumor mill works. I asked what the "protest" was about, and no one really seemed to know. Because the vast majority of the people were familiar with the school and the process that made it a reality, many expressed surprise at the sight of the placards and pamphlets. Because the original plan was to have a ribbon-cutting ceremony with the hunger strikers in tow, it didn't make too much sense that community members would be staging a protest. As Rito (principal of the Social Justice High School), shrugged shoulders in the hallway about what was going on, we went about the day. However, I couldn't get it out of my mind: Why the signs and placards?

Like many experiences in teaching, the process of reflection can offer tangible solutions. Later in the day, while standing in a corridor of vending machines at the university where I teach, I ran into one of the hunger strikers. She and I were making small talk about the first day at the high school. "Oh, so you were there too?" she asked. When I replied yes, I also mentioned that I saw two of the huelgistas *in the service drive holding a sign and passing out pamphlets. Before I could ask a question about what I perceived to be a protest, she informed me that, "We just wanted to greet families and remind them of why the school was built and of our availability to them if they had questions for us." She also told me that they wanted to develop a parent center that would be accessible to the parents of the students and the community at large. In my mind I was puzzled for about twenty seconds, and then it dawned on me: what I thought to be a protest was actually the* huelgistas *welcoming students and parents to the high school! By this time, while wallowing in my own ignorance, the importance of the work I originally set out to do would smack me in the face. Before assuming, one must listen. Only from these spaces will we gain understanding.*

～

The opening counterstory is representative of the stumbles and mistakes I've made during my personal journey in working with the collective of community members, teachers, families, and community organizations that were instrumental in creating SOJO. In order to make sense of the aforementioned complex, interwoven layers of race, place, and school, the following chapter seeks to provide context for the creation of the high school. Critical to this framing is the political and sociohistorical contexts of both neighborhoods, the initial story of the hunger strike, and the political economy of CPS. As an overarching theme, the influence of neoliberal urbanism is vital to understanding the current political moment in CPS and in the city writ large. Additionally, my own position as a researcher/educator is perpetually questioned in a process where I participated in the development of mission, vision, school culture, and curriculum for a high school. From my perspective, the questioning of positionality is a good and necessary thing. Because researchers are traditionally trained to distance themselves from the "research site," we fall victim to the false colonial notion of academic "objectivity" (Thuiwai-Smith, 2012). In the attempt to create research "from a distance," we move further away from grasping with the "messiness" of human life. Fortunately and unfortunately for us, our lives are not perfect, clean, and ordered spaces—they are never objective. In this instance, these murky, contested, difficult, and affirming spaces pose unique challenges at any given moment in time.

It is from this perspective that I try to understand myself as a person working with young people and families in La Villita and North Lawndale. Positioned against mainstream media iterations of gang infestation, open-air drug markets, and despair in both communities, there is another story beneath the surface. At first glance, both communities are definitively unique. La Villita has a bustling business corridor and is one of the most densely populated communities in Chicago. North Lawndale, on the other hand, is one of the more sparsely populated communities in the city, at one time having more vacant lots than any other neighborhood in Chicago. Simultaneously, North Lawndale has the highest concentration of greystone buildings, which are some of the most highly coveted properties in the city due to their significance as present remnants of the turn-of-the-century Chicago school of architecture. However, in light of their distinct characteristics on the exterior, both communities share a historical and structural narrative as the community of Greater Lawndale. Deeply rooted in the ideology and practice of White supremacy/racism and neoliberalism, both communities rest firmly in the contradictions of community renewal and disinvestment. As ideology and practice, White supremacy/racism provides an alternate lens by which to assess issues and concerns in both spaces. Combined with the machinations of the neoliberal state, both communities have intimate relationships with particular forms of disinvestment, marginalization, and isolation. Although most visible in North Lawndale, White flight operated at a slower pace in La Villita due to initial attempts of inclusion by long-term White residents. Explained in detail throughout the following sections, the structural and ideological tropes of White supremacy/racism deeply impact each other, promoting aversion between members in both communities. To their credit, some residents of both communities understood this relationship and refused the engineered xenophobia between both neighborhoods outright. Nevertheless, despite many tension-filled moments throughout our process on SOJO's design team, it is in the spirit of those forward-thinking community residents, that the high school was imagined.

Interest Convergence in the City:
Chicago as Metaphor for Neoliberal Urban Education "Reform"

Coined by legal scholar Derrick Bell (1930–2011), the concept of interest convergence has particular importance in relation to neoliberal urbanism and educational policy in Chicago. The idea that the larger mainstream White society will only accommodate racial equity when it is to their advantage is critical in understanding education and housing policy in Chicago (Bell 1980, 523). In Chicago, because advancements in racial justice have proved beneficial for a small population of middle-class and affluent African-American and Latino/a residents, the vast majority of said populations are still reeling from neoliberal housing and education policy in the city. Documented extensively in the works of Lipman (2003, 2004, 2011), Saltman (2007, 2009), and Fine and Fabricant (2012), Chicago has been a hotbed for educational "reforms." Where changes have been touted as positive, in actuality they have largely resulted in further marginalization of low-income, working-class communities of color throughout the city. It becomes important to frame the hunger strike and the subsequent formation of SOJO in the context of Chicago and neoliberal urbanism, as the city has been centered in the rhetoric of "competition," "value added," and "research driven" in relation to workforce development and education. As part of the politics of interruption, the members of the communities of North Lawndale and Little Village vehemently oppose the neoliberal turn in education. From the federal policy of No Child Left Behind (NCLB) to its localized manifestation through Renaissance 2010, SOJO exists in a complex intersection of community demand, education policy, community development, and partisan politics. Where these types of entanglements are familiar to Chicago, the intersection deserves attention in order to understand the relationship between hypersegregation, neoliberal urbanism, and educational policy.

Rooted in the belief that free-market economies provide solutions to the vast majority of social concerns, neoliberal reform is centered in the rights of the individual coupled with the privatization of public goods. The market is understood as correct and without fault, resulting in the rationale for privatization of public goods for the purpose of cost-effectiveness and the maximizing of profits. Through these machinations neoliberal policies "have succeeded in reshaping cities and urban policy discourses and have set in motion new forms of economic, social, and spatial inequality, marginality and exclusion" (Lipman 2011, 26). For low-income families of color, this often results in a rhetorical charge that the market can solve the vast majority of political, economic, and social issues. Because these resources are falsely positioned as available to all, low-income, working-class families of color are often blamed for not accessing said resources.

This manifestation is glaringly evident in Chicago. Centered in the 1995 educational policy shift resulting in mayoral control of CPS, the mayor currently has sole authority in appointing the school board, which is responsible for final approval of school-related issues (e.g., financial matters, curricular shifts, contract procurement, approval of new schools, etc). In addition to the ability to appoint members of the school board, the mayor has the ability to overturn any decision made by the board. Facilitated under the twenty-two-year mayoral tenure of Richard J. Daley, the city has laid a blueprint for numerous cities in the United States desiring to centralize control of its school system. In that time frame, the number of educators on the school board has decreased significantly. Currently the board membership consists largely of people from business, legal, and philanthropic sectors. This fosters a reciprocal relationship between the board and the mayor's office as board members are usually individuals or employees of entities who have contributed significantly to the mayor's reelection campaign.

Deeply rooted in neoliberal ideology and rhetoric, this facilitated convergence of housing and educational policies. With Chicago's attempt to market itself as a global city, housing has been paired with education as key components in the city's development, while attracting international investment from tourism and business ventures. Dating back to 1971, mayor Richard J. Daley (father of Richard M.) spearheaded a policy and planning initiative known as the Chicago 21 Plan, targeting twenty-one wards (geographic and political districts) for redevelopment. Considered as part of the last wave of urban renewal strategies, the Chicago 21 Plan should be understood as the blueprint for neoliberal reform in the city.

Fast-forwarding forty-plus years to the present, actions by the mayor and other state agencies to secure corporate contributions via free-market strategies has become the norm not only locally, but nationally and internationally. Sections of the Chicago model of reform have been duplicated in cities like New York, Los Angeles, and Houston. Officials from all three cities have come to Chicago to study mayoral control (of the school board) and how to connect education and business with the intent to foster long-term development. Internationally Chicago has been cited for its improvements in business, housing, and education. As a central hub for global finance, informational technological advancements, and management for systems of production, Chicago has fashioned itself as a viable competitor for investment from transnational global firms in business, industry, and entertainment (Smith and Stovall, 2008).

Through a collaborative of business interests known as the Commercial Club of Chicago, its Civic Committee developed a 2003 report known as "Left Behind." Included in this report was the notion that students in the United States were falling behind internationally in reading, math, and science. Their suggested solution was to retool the public educational landscape by infusing "innovation" from the business sector. Said innovations would be for the purposes of strengthening the US workforce and returning the US economy to supremacy in the global marketplace. The people best suited for this direction were those who possessed an intimate knowledge of free-market strategies to boost competition among education providers (Civic Committee of the Commercial Club of Chicago, 2003). Key to this strategy is the idea that competition is best to boost academic performance. Under free-market capitalism the belief is that if one school is performing well, it will push others to improve due to the interests of both institutions for students. Contrary to this understanding is the fact that each school serves a different set of students requiring a unique set of resources germane to that particular population. The market-based competition strategy becomes ridiculous and absurd when accounting for the unique needs of students in a particular school.

Nevertheless, the city moved forward with the policy and rolled out a plan in the summer of 2004 called Renaissance 2010. Discussed in detail in chapter 3, the idea promoted to the public was to implement the suggestions of the Civic Committee. In Chicago and other large urban centers in the United States for now and the foreseeable future, public education is intimately connected to market-driven neoliberal urbanism. Discussed in detail in the next sections, this reality was inescapable in our duration on the design team. SOJO, as a neighborhood public school, exists in perpetually contested space as a school that comes into existence during the height of the Plan for Transformation and Renaissance 2010. As the two policies converge, they provide the backdrop for the historical undergirding of the politics of interruption in creating a neighborhood high school.

Greater Lawndale in Context:
La Villita (South Lawndale) and North Lawndale

Chicago, as a city hypersegregated by race and class, contains many adjacent neighborhoods that have strict, understood, physical and psychological boundaries that limit interactions between different racial/ethnic and socioeconomic groups. Despite the adjacent relationship and similar economic narratives, there are situations where the physical, psychic, and historical boundaries prohibit residents from traveling outside of their demarcated space. Language, race, culture, and geography continue to expand the complexities of space in both neighborhoods to this day. However, there have been intentional moments of engagement, from the election of Harold Washington in 1983, the creation of the Independent Political Organization (IPO) in 1981, and numerous conjoined efforts for accessible transportation and community development in the late 1990s and early twenty-first century (i.e., the development of the Pink Line rail system that services both communities). The creation of the high school should be included in the continuum of such developments.

Often relegated to the historical memory of long-term Chicago residents, the neighborhoods of South Lawndale/Little Village (La Villita) and North Lawndale were at one time known as the Community of Greater Lawndale. The monikers of North and South come in later years as the two communities began to divide geographically and ethnically. Until the mid-1940s North Lawndale remained primarily populated by the descendants of Jewish families largely from Russia while the South remained a stronghold for residents of Hungarian, Ukrainian, and Czech heritage. Over the years, demographic shifts precipitated by deindustrialization and urban sprawl (particularly suburbanization and White flight) resulted in marginalization and isolation for both communities. Because it was not as heavily affected by the 1968 riots after Martin Luther King Jr.'s assassination, South Lawndale's racial transition was slower, but in the end, both communities became predominantly communities of color. Despite the slower rate of transition for South Lawndale, the overarching narrative of both communities is similar. However, the realities of neighborhood transition and subsequent development have manifested themselves differently in both spaces.

Simultaneously, the two communities are continually pegged as largely poverty-stricken and devoid of concerned residents. Never to discount the challenges faced by members of both communities (i.e., poverty, illicit drug trade proliferation, street organization (gang) tensions, police brutality, disinvestment, destabilization, marginalization, isolation, etc.), more nuanced accounts of community dynamics are critical in locating critical undercurrents of resistance and struggle. On closer review, both communities have been ravaged by policies rooted in a logic of disposability. As critical infrastructure has either been removed or is significantly difficult to access in both communities, many residents are relegated to matrix of survival-mode, making it difficult to move beyond immediate needs. Returning to neoliberal rhetoric, the city has access to a population that is disposable, meaning it can be instantly replaced due to the extreme difficulty in securing quality of life concerns (i.e., housing and schools). With few alternatives, the hope is that a rotating door of new residents will not be able to organize due to the immediate difficulties of making it through the day.

Fortunately history has provided another narrative. It is from these struggles that communities galvanize their efforts to pose new alternatives with the intent of changing their conditions. Significant factions in La Villita and North Lawndale have been diligent in their resistance to state violence in the form of housing discrimination, inequitable education, low-wage employment, and access to health care. Although organizing in both communities has largely occurred separately, the brief moments of collaborative community organizing between both communities provide the counternarrative to commonplace rhetoric of disposability through blight and abandonment.

Recognizing explicit challenges in both communities, there is another layer that pairs and separates both communities. Although not the focus of this book, the nonprofit industrial complex (NPIC) plays a significant role in the development of the high school. Deeply centered in two community development corporations and one philanthropic organization, all three were instrumental to the school's development. Nevertheless, there are internal and external contradictions that are important to the history and future of both neighborhoods. The Little Village Community Development Corporation (LVCDC), the Lawndale Community Development Corporation (LCDC) and the Steans Family Foundation were instrumental in the early organization and development of the design teams and the subsequent creation of the high school. LVCDC and LCDC, as community development corporations operate as a hub for community initiatives that are centered in community needs, often training and employing community residents as facilitators of the various initiatives. While not "corporations" in the traditional sense, they are outgrowth of the advent of community organizations originally centered in housing and commercial development. As a outgrowth of the Ford Foundation's 1960 Gray Areas Program, the Federal

Government's Special Impact Program, and the 1966 amendment to the 1964 Economic Opportunity Act, CDCs are loosely defined as organizations that are "private, non-profit development organizations, serve low and moderate income people and their communities, have a community-based board and have completed at least one unit of housing or one commercial or industrial development project" (National Congress of Community Economic Development in Liou and Smith, 1996, 2). Both organizations, developed to address community needs, find themselves in a particular daily internal struggle. Because the two establishments are heavily supported by philanthropic organizations, the fact of perpetually shifting funding priorities has the potential to place them at the behest of their funders. In both instances, program coordinators and executive directors find themselves in the perpetual grind of attempting to secure multiyear grants that may or may not be centered in the needs of the community.

The Steans Family Foundation, as a philanthropic organization that focuses specifically on North Lawndale, operates from a different perspective. Harrison Steans made his money with a corporation that bought banks and later founded the Financial Investments Corporation of Chicago, specializing in venture capital and real estate. He also founded North Lawndale College Prep in 1998 and has a daughter who sits on the board (Fortin 1998). As a grant-awarding organization, they define themselves as "investors" in North Lawndale, "interested in creating the highest possible levels of human gain for the limited dollars we have available" (www.steansfamily-foundation.org/principles.shtml). Again, the free-market neoliberal rhetoric is important, as many Steans awardees in education are charter schools. This becomes important because charters are viewed as contributors to educational "innovation" in relation to their results-based strategies. At the same time, included in their awardees are other local organizations that are engaged in work with some of the most marginalized members of the community of North Lawndale. Organizationally, these tensions are both racialized and classed. The Steans family is a wealthy White family from an affluent Chicago suburb. One hundred percent of their grantees serve students of color (primarily African-American) in North Lawndale. Similar to philanthropist Julius Rosenwald in the development of rural schools and historical Black Colleges and Universities (HBCUs) in the early twentieth century, the Steans foundation are similiar White architects of Black education, in that their efforts may be charitably motivated, but are not centered in creating self-sufficient communities (Watkins, 2004). Instead, their grant-making is still an act of benevolence, disallowing grantees to ask and answer deeper questions about their conditions and how to change them.

At the same time, there are scores of North Lawndale residents who would defend the work of the Steans Family Foundation. Some feel that if not for their efforts, many of the programs centered in community uplift would not exist. As a structural issue, I cannot discount their agency and navigational skills that allow them the ability to develop concrete analysis of their condition while moving to improve it. For these reasons, I do not posit that the founders of the Steans Foundation are inherently bad people. Instead, I see their efforts as reflective of a misinformed, missionary mentality based in market-driven strategies. Business models of education are problematic in that winners and losers are often predetermined. If we have schools that focus on college admission as the sole model of success, rationales are created to dismiss those who are not thought to be a "fit." This returns us back to the colonizer rationale of "we know what's best for you." Because this is incorrect, it would be egregious to write a story absent of these tensions. The NPIC does not evoke a linear, causal relationship between the organization, its grantees, and the communities they serve. Because the tensions are layered and complex, the responsibility of the Critical Race Scholar is to name the contestation outright, with a commitment to unpack the contradictions for the purpose of improving future work. In relation to SOJO, certain staff members of the Steans Foundation, in partnership with the Bill and Melinda Gates Foundation through the Chicago High School Redesign Initiative (CHSRI), were instrumental to the design team in our process and beyond opening day.

Coupling the relationship of community development corporations to the NPIC, LVCDC, and LCDC share a connection through the Local Initiatives Support Corporation (LISC), which has been instrumental in various initiatives in North Lawndale and La Villita. Adding education to the original tropes of housing and commercial development, the efforts of LISC are funded by major national philanthropic organizations (e.g., the Ford Foundation, MacArthur Foundation, McCormick Foundation, etc.) and corporate sponsors (e.g., J. P. Morgan Chase Bank). Where the corporate relationships are not guaranteed to devalue the work that is happening on the ground with communities, they can be influential regarding the direction and limitation of the community engagement. Deepening the contradictions, in the process of creating design teams, several key members of the creation of the high school process were unable to continue with the process due to lack of funding. Discussed in future chapters, the NPIC relationship, in the case of LVCDC and LCDC, is indicative of an uneven relationship that has resulted in both contested constraint and tangible community development. Throughout my involvement on the design team and into the life of SOJO, these contestations are ever present.

La Villita: Transition, Struggle, and Community Stability

Originally conceptualized as a subdivision of suburban Cicero by real estate developers Alden C. Millard and Edwin Decker in 1871, as an area for affluent families, Lawndale soon shifted to a predominantly working-class community by the turn of the century. As the West side of the city became the hub of early twentieth century industry for Chicago and the Midwest region, affluent German and Irish descended residents were replaced by Czech, Polish, German, and Hungarian immigrants seeking work in the industrial sector (Magallon 2009, 9).

For years, South Lawndale (then known as Lawndale/Crawford) became a desired community, as the neighborhood of Pilsen contained overcrowded tenement apartments populated with first-generation Eastern European immigrants. As well-paying factory and city employment became available for the sons and daughters of the first generation, families began to move south and purchased smaller, single-family brick homes that were reflective of the community's working-class ilk. Large factories like Western Electric and International Harvester employed thousands of residents, creating a staple of secure employment for two generations of families. Additionally, the business corridor on Twenty-Sixth Street provided opportunities for families who sought to branch out from factory jobs into entrepreneurial ventures. This created a vibrant, working-class community that was able to maintain itself and continue the tradition of Chicago as a "city of neighborhoods." Missing from this narrative, however, was the residential segregation of the city that contained thousands of African-Americans on the South Side of the city. Although their migration west to North Lawndale would soon follow, the peaceful imagery of early- to mid-twentieth-century South Lawndale as Eastern European ethnic enclave is a popular narrative in Chicago lore. However, the Eastern European iteration of the story only provides a partial view into the layered complexities of the neighborhood.

Although the community is largely thought to be a space that made a smooth transition from White Eastern European residents to a predominantly Latino/a enclave, the shift reveals deeper contestation. By the 1950s, Latino/a families began to locate in South Lawndale in small numbers in the northeastern portion of the neighborhood. Thought of as a natural extension of Pilsen (the adjacent community to the North and East), these families also had members who were able to secure employment or embark on entrepreneurial ventures in the city. Pilsen, also making a transition from Eastern European to Latino/a (predominantly Mexican) was densely popu-lated and had little room for new residents at the time. Additionally, the neighborhood directly to the North of Pilsen (Little Italy) had a growing number of Latino/a families by the late 1950s (Fernandez, 2012). By the mid-1960s, these families were displaced by the building of the University of Illinois at Chicago East Campus, razing thousands of homes in favor of university buildings. Many of these displaced families sought refuge in South Lawndale, as second- and third-generation Whites who could afford it were moving out of the neighborhood for larger homes in newly sprawling suburbs to the North and West. Because the numbers were relatively small at first, Latino/a families were able to move into Lawndale with minimal infractions. In fact, there were attempts at inclusion that were relatively suc-cessful as the name "Little Village" was coined by president Richard Dolejs of the Twenty-Sixth Street Community Council reflect immigrant families from Czechoslovakia, Yugoslavia, Hungary, Ukraine, and Mexico. The idea was that families with roots in the aforementioned countries were most familiar with smaller towns or "villages" (Magallon 2010, 91).

By the same token, the inclusion of Latino/a families was largely rooted in the Twenty-Sixth Street Council's attempt to disassociate them-selves from the African-American neighborhood of North Lawndale. This slowly began the divide between Latino/a and African-American residents, largely fueled by racial animus from the descendants of Eastern Europeans. As North Lawndale was given the nickname "Slumdale" by White residents in the early '60s, there was fear that South Lawndale would succumb to the same conditions as their northern neighbors. Latino/a residents, firmly estab-lished in the northeast corner of the community, were positioned as hard-working families who had come quietly to the neighborhood. Despite their "deserving" status granted by ethnic Whites, this was a shrouded attempt to preserve established businesses on Twenty-Sixth Street. For these reasons, community stabilization became critical. In order to do so, it became criti-cally important to establish relationships with the newly growing community of Latino/a residents. Despite the initial delay of White flight, the combina-tion of the draw of the suburbs coupled with the fear of the encroachment of new African-American residents to the North, changed the community for good. As these families slowly left the neighborhood, their businesses went with them. However, instead of the buildings lying dormant, enterprising Latino/a residents purchased or leased many of the storefronts and replaced existing establishments with taquerias, *carnecerias*, *supermercados*, *botanicas*, and restaurants from Northern and Central Mexican states. Still known by many as Little Village, many residents have adopted the nickname "La Villita," to reflect the culture of its current population (ibid.). Shrouded in the veneer of cultural tourism and historical nostalgia, the retail corridor of Twenty-Sixth Street in La Villita is currently positioned as a tourist destination for visitors to Chicago. Due to its insular and densely populated corridors, Twenty-Sixth Street is the second-highest-grossing retail district in the city of Chicago (Magallon 2009, 10).

At the same time, the community remains a hub for immigrant families that may not reap the benefits of the economic virility of Twenty-Sixth Street. Internally, this has created a partial rift. While the majority of the community would be considered working class/low income, there are small sections of the community that have middle-class enclaves. Largely fueled by the aforementioned economic gains by a slight number of residents, these have made for divisions in the community regarding education, housing, and city services. Specifically in education, this has created tensions as to what type of schools best serve community members. As there is a significant push locally and nationally for charter schools, organizations like the United Neighborhood Organization have championed the proliferation of charters to address the shortfalls of CPS in providing quality education for working-class and low-income Latino/a families. Complicating matters further, as some residents gained financial stability, they also moved to adjacent suburban communities, further depleting the community's tax base. The neighboring suburbs of Cicero, Stickney, and Berwyn, like La Villita, have shifted from predominantly White to Latino/a. In light of these factors, there continues to be concerted efforts to address the needs of community residents in La Villita.

North Lawndale:
Containment, Destabilization, and the Will to Fight

Rapidly dwindling numbers of North Lawndale residents and even fewer Chicagoans remember the community as a thriving, robust port of entry for Russian Jews. Instead, the common narrative filling popular news outlets is one of blight and neglect. At the same time, in opposition to the commonplace narrative, it is important to understand the dynamics of North Lawndale as imbued in a larger story of racial animus, deindustrialization, disinvestment, exploitation, and active resistance through community organizing. In recognition of these factors, it is also important to understand North Lawndale structurally. From a structural perspective, we can conclude that "slum" conditions are not an inherent occurrence. Rather, they are intimately connected to the political, social, and economic moments, through individual and collective actions that contribute to a neighborhood's decline. Resisting this narrative, the history of community organizing in North Lawndale sheds a different light on the community. Instead of a neighborhood that experienced decline completely at the behest of its new residents, it was a space targeted for containment and marginalization by the state (the "state" in this instance being the city of Chicago).

Annexed by the city in 1889, North Lawndale was originally an extension of the township of Cicero. Marked as an industrial area, international companies established plants that served as the economic engine for the community until the mid-twentieth century. With the influx of factories to the community, none was more influential than the World Headquarters of the Sears & Roebuck Company. With an expansive footprint on the community, headquarters provided workers with a community center, health clinic, parks and recreation services, and athletic fields (Lane et al. 2007, 4).

The golden years of North Lawndale's economic boon (1900–1950) were also a period of intense population growth, as the community's population doubled from 1910 to 1920 and added an additional 18,000 residents by 1930 (Lane et al., 5). In the decade of 1950–1960, however, many factories began to downsize while some relocated to other areas in the city and suburbs. During the same time period, the population almost shifted completely from 90 percent Jewish in 1950 to 91 percent African-American by 1965. Sears & Roebuck Co. followed suit, relocating their operations to the suburbs, with the North Lawndale World Headquarters center officially shutting its doors by 1987. By the mid-1950s, African-American residents began to descend on the community as restrictive covenants on home ownership and rentals were lifted throughout the city. Coming in on the tail end of the second stint of the Great Migration, the influx of this new group of residents were also largely from the South. Paired with residents from the South Side of the city, the abundance of housing stock presented new opportunities for families in a neighborhood that was steadily depopulating. At the same time, with the departure of large industry came significant unemployment, creating significant decreases in social and economic infrastructure (Lane et al., 6).

Deeping the socioeconomic challenges to the community was the predatory lending practice of contract sales. Due to the ability to gain steady factory employment in the community or in one of the nearby collar suburbs, some African-American migrants to North Lawndale were able to purchase homes. However, these purchases were dubious, due to the exploitative nature of contract sales. Similar to the housing bubble of the early twentieth-first century, with the advent of Adjustable Rate Mortgages (ARM) and other dubious financial instruments like credit default swaps, contract sales were in the same vein. Masterfully explained by Satter in her account for the struggle for fair housing throughout Chicago's West Side, this practice was the amalgamation of racist exclusion from the Federal Housing Authority (FHA), the City of Chicago, and the Mortgage Lenders Association.

> Because Blacks were excluded from conventional sources of mortgage financing, they were forced to buy on contract. But installment land contracts (or "articles of agreement for warranty deed," as they were technically called) left buyers . . . in a highly vulnerable position. Like homeowners, they were responsible for insurance and upkeep—but like renters they could be thrown out if they missed a payment. While it cost from $100 to $300 to instigate foreclosure proceedings against those defaulting on a mortgage, a forcible entry and detainer (that is, eviction) action against a contract buyer cost only $4.50. Worst of all, evictions in Illinois were extraordinarily difficult to challenge in court. (Satter 2009, 57)

The process of renting apartments was no better. With the decline of large industry in the neighborhood, housing stock was turned over to slumlords who did little to nothing in terms of upkeep and repairs. Unlike South Lawndale, Jewish residents in the first decade of the twentieth century built large, multiunit apartment buildings to address overcrowding, as families rapidly populated the neighborhood. As these families moved to suburbs and other parts of the city, some saw seized on money-making opportunities. If they could "flip" some apartment buildings (buy them and sell them after one year to make a profit), it would also leave them money to buy other properties and rent them out as income property. Because the neighborhood remained overcrowded with the surge of Black families, rents were inflated due to limited housing options for poor residents and the lack of public housing stock in the community. These factors enabled slumlords to charge exorbitant prices for rent while refusing to tend to basic maintenance and upkeep. As apartment buildings remained in disrepair, vermin infestations, and other health concerns became rampant.Further contributing to the mainstream narrative of blight and neglect is the idea that the community never recovered from the 1968 riots in protest of Dr. King's assassination. While this is partially accurate, under closer examination, predating King's arrival in 1966, factors contributing to disinvestment and community desta-bilization were firmly in play. Noting the rapid economic decline of North Lawndale beginning in the mid-1950s, the Southern Christian Leadership Conference (SCLC) targeted the neighborhood as part of its "Northern campaign" (Satter 2009, 172). As King and members of the SCLC were amazed at the issues facing North Lawndale, they observed the proliferation of contract sales in the purchasing of homes (180).

Again, the common narrative is one of residential neglect mainly per-petrated by community residents. On the contrary, the story remains com-plex and varied. North Lawndale, as a community of new Black migrants, was blamed for a process of blight that they neither started nor were assisted by the city in changing. Instead, state sanctioned practices of isolation and marginalization, buttressed by substandard education, proximal access to low-wage service sector employment, and predatory lending practices in home purchases and apartment rentals were central in keeping African-American residents of North Lawndale in survival mode. Because rents and mortgages were essentially unaffordable, residents with jobs often had to take up multiple employment just to keep up with rent and mortgage payments. This makes for little time to engage in upkeep and maintenance of housing stock. Coupled with a second stint of outward migration beginning in the 1970s, the community had little time to recover. Captured succinctly by Klinenberg in his description of the 1995 heat wave that ravaged the com-munity, similar conditions prevailed for almost twenty years later.

> With few jobs, stores or other public amenities to attract them to the area and a depleted infrastructure after the 1968 riots, the more mobile North Lawndale residents fled the area—almost as quickly as the local Jewish population had a few decades before. Between 1970 and 1990, roughly one-half migrated outward, leaving behind empty homes as well as the neighbors who were either committed or condemned to stay. (Klinenberg 2002, 95)

Discussed in detail later in this chapter, neoliberalism rests the burden of the condition of a community as primarily the fault of the individual. Embedded in the rhetoric of "if the community really cared, then they would take charge of the situation," this common trope deserves to be chal-lenged as historically false and damaging. As its historic Jewish population left for greener pastures in other parts of the city and sprawling suburbs, Black residents of North Lawndale were immersed in a community that left minimal access to infrastructure and employment. The process continues to this day as residents and organizations in the area have had little time to engage in individual and collective healing from the trauma of long-term disinvestment and community upheaval.

Over the last sixty years Lawndale has experienced two out-migrations of human and physical resources. In addition to the out-migration of Jewish families in the mid-1950s and mid-1960s, there was a second outward migration of African-American residents in the early 1980s to mid-1990s, who left for more desirable neighborhoods. Despite the colossal costs to the community, there are still efforts aimed at reinvigoration and stability. At the same time, it is incorrect to position North Lawndale residents as hapless victims. Historically and to this day there are numerous organizations that have dedicated themselves to the development and further improvement of the community. From the Contract Buyers of Lawndale (CBL) in the late 1960s to the North Lawndale News, to the Lawndale Christian Development Organization developed in 1987, despite challenging circumstances, they have been attempts to develop infrastructure throughout the community. Beginning with the Contract Buyers League in the late 1960s and early '70s, and efforts to address school overcrowding in the '80s, these moments of organizing have been riddled with infrastructure deterioration and massive disinvestment.

Imbedded in this process and deeply critical to the development of the high school was previously mentioned Lawndale Christian Development Corporation (LCDC). Started as the extension of a Lawndale Christian Church in 1987, its expansion to a community development corporation has centered itself in education, housing, employment, and health care. When community development corporations became the darlings of the philanthropic sector in the early 2000s, LCDC was able to capitalize on this moment while building infrastructure along the Ogden corridor (one of the two major thoroughfares in the neighborhood). Devastated by the '68 riots, Ogden Avenue laid barren for years, with few business outlets and even fewer homes. As the church settled on Ogden, one of the goals was to positively affect development on the corridor. Over the last twenty years this has resulted in a bustling section on Ogden that spans over half a mile on both sides of the street. Housed in their development are a café, a health care center, an early childhood training center, several rooms available to the community for rentals, a partnership with a local restaurant, several community centers with exercise facilities, a senior citizens center, and a employment center. Paired with housing development in housing with city-assisted greystone preservation, and new housing development, there has been a concerted effort to address some of the definitive issues in the neighborhood.

In addition to organizations like LCDC, the Homan Square organization is the outgrowth of a public partnership between business, city, and community interests. Located on the site of the former world headquarters for Sears, Roebuck & Company, the development features apartments, townhomes, a retail strip mall anchored by a grocery store and a cinema, a charter school, and community center. Originally thought to be the linchpin in the redevelopment effort in North Lawndale, the effort was welcomed by the community. However the issue is still one of access, in that to qualify for housing in Homan Square, one must be "lease compliant" and have no felonies or history of drug abuse. As a beautification effort, it serves as a section of the community that has the potential for access, but could also be viewed with disdain as this is yet another attempt to exclude those who have been historically excluded from access to housing, health care and gainful employment.

One of the more controversial developments in North Lawndale since the late 1990s has been the proliferation of charter schools. Originally, positioned in the community to address historic disinvestment in schools by CPS, they were originally envisioned as a viable tool for educational process in the neighborhood. Before the wide-scale proliferation of charters in Illinois and throughout the country, North Lawndale housed some of the first charters in the city, beginning with North Lawndale College Prep (NCLP). Envisioned in the original version of the concept that allowed for teacher innovation, student agency, and family input, charters were originally thought to provide a pathway to viable educational options for the community. As this vision was short-lived nationally, it had an even shorter shelf life in Chicago. Nevertheless, the tide of charters took hold in the neighborhood, resulting in the depopulation of neighborhood public schools in the area. The groundswell of community support was rooted in the fact that educational options for Black youth in North Lawndale were slim due to nearly six decades of disinvestment from CPS. Similar to the situation in New Orleans, the remaining families are sold the idea that "you've had sixty-plus years of madness, so let us provide you with something new" (Buras 2009). However, coupled with this backstory is the fact that many of the charter developments were not equipped to address the expressed needs of the community. Using the neoliberal marketplace ideology of students and parents as "customers," this ideology has resulted in hyperreliance on high-stakes standardized test scores as the sole purveyor of educational achievement (Fine and Fabricant, 2011). One prominent national educational management organization (EMO), KIPP Inc. had a school in North Lawndale that closed its doors in the late 2000s. NCLP has expanded to the former Collins high school, while another charter has opened its doors in the former Mason elementary school, once an anchor to the North Lawndale community.

The public-private partnership between CPS and local community organizations were envisioned as key to developing sustainable educational models that addressed student needs through relevant curriculum. As test scores on standardized tests are no real sign of educational attainment or improvement, the suspension rates and expulsion rates for charters and CPS schools are similar, with charters surpassing CPS schools in expulsions and suspensions (Ahmed-Ullah and Richards 2014).

Resisting the Machine: Community Organizing and Electoral Politics in North Lawndale and La Villita

From the struggle to develop bilingual education programs in CPS, to securing Latino/a representation in City Hall and the Illinois Legislature, to supporting the election of Chicago's first African-American mayor, La Villita has a rich history of community activism. For the myriad reasons, the events leading to the hunger strike beginning on May 13, 2001 should be included in the trajectory of community activism, amid the politically charged realities of Chicago. Often left to the memory of community members, there has been a recent surge of scholarship regarding community struggle for quality education in Chicago (Danns 2004, Lipman 2011, Kartemquin Films, 2014). Almost thirty years prior to the hunger strike, the neighboring Latino/a community to the northeast of La Villita known as Pilsen engaged in a community struggle to build what is now Benito Juarez High School (Cortez 2008, 24). In the late 1960s, African-American residents in North Lawndale engaged in community struggle to get Black studies classes at Farragut High School and to create Collins Community High School in the early 1980s.

At the same time, competing political and community interests in La Villita are critical to the discussion of school creation. Internally and externally, competing interests at the neighborhood level create instances where the purpose of education is perpetually in question. For some, there is a push to make sure that education is the tool for assimilation, making sure that Latino/a families have access to an "American Dream." For others, education is the tool to make informed decisions on your life, while seeking to improve the conditions of your community at the collective and individual level. While many would argue the fact that there is overlap in both stances, the differences are fundamental as various factions position themselves as "authentic" voices for the Latino/a community.

All of these tensions are visible in the struggle for community power. Because the majority of political power in Chicago is centralized in the mayor's office, many local officials (in this case aldermen) feel it is in their best interest to acquiesce to the whims of the mayor. Although the modus operandi of many elected officials in Chicago's fifty aldermanic wards, the twenty-second ward (home to La Villita) operates as a hotbed of resistance to the mayor's demands. Simultaneously, it is not a sanguine resistance by community members under the same ideological banner. Instead, there are those who still side with "the machine" and those who choose to oppose it, citing structural and ideological differences with the mayor's office. These ideological differences come to a head when questions of community infrastructure (particularly housing, education, and employment) are at play. Nevertheless, opposition to traditional machine politics has made the twenty-second ward an outlier over the last thirty-plus years. Despite encroaching internal and external pressures to comply, the hunger strike is an extension of consistent resistance to the will of the mayor's office.

As the community shifted racially from White to Latino/a, members of the community began to notice disinvestment from the mayor's office. Known locally and nationally as "the machine," Chicago is steeped in a decades-long history of democratic power-wielding that specifically rests power at the mayor's bequest. Throughout my time on the design team, understanding electoral and community politics of La Villita were vital to my personal political education. Gaining a deeper understanding of the struggle for community control allowed for me navigate through the perpetually shifting contexts at the individual, organizational, and electoral level.

Rooted in the activism of the Independent Political Organization (IPO) under the leadership of Rudy Lozano (1951–1983), Jesus "Chuy" Garcia, and Linda Coronado, Little Village residents saw it necessary to break ties with the political machine of Chicago. Under Richard J. Daley's terms as mayor in the city, La Villita witnessed the removal or tapering of critical central infrastructure (street cleaning, street light repair, garbage pickup, etc.). After Daley's death, the two subsequent mayors did little to support infrastructure in the community, continuing the process of disinvestment. Because residents were not beholden to the mayor and the loyal white residents had since relocated to the suburbs, Daley saw no reason to afford La Villita the services it was accustomed to seeing. From these spaces, Lozano and others sought to push back against central office, demanding services and representation for Latinos/as in local government. Culminating in a failed bid for city council and his untimely murder, the work of the IPO under Lozano galvanized the community to push for progressive, representative government.

Similar to the attempts made during the design team process, the IPO also sought to develop a coalition with the African-American community through their elected officials. Because African-American communities were also bearing the brunt of disinvestment and marginalization, members of the IPO felt as if there was a logical alliance between both racial groups to rise against the whims of the mayor. Initially this coalition included prominent African-American politicians Harold Washington, Danny Davis, and Bobby Rush (Cortez 2008, 28). Understanding their frustration with the mayor's office, the idea was to develop a united front to secure resources for African-American and Latino/a neighborhoods. Because of the unfamiliarity with each other, it was difficult to get support for such a coalition. In a city so heavily controlled by the mayor, many elected officials and community members get caught in the illusion of limited resources and only engage each other only to the extent that they can garner votes. Paired with the deeply rooted racism engendered by decades of regional hypersegregation, the challenges are formidable. Nevertheless, this coalition was instrumental in the mayoral elections of 1983 and 1987, resulting in victories for Harold Washington. Although the coalition was short-lived due to mayor Washington's untimely death, it stands as the symbol of possibility.

Briefly proceeding and shortly after the Washington campaign, another organization came into prominence, deepening tensions as it made the switch from community organization to a professional establishment centered in the development of the Latino/a professional class. Founded in 1980 in the Neighborhood of South Chicago, the United Neighborhood Organization (UNO) originally set out to connect the power of organized labor and churches to guarantee basic services for Mexican residents in disinvested neighborhoods (Cortez 2008, 35). By the time one of its founding members (Danny Solis) transitioned from leadership in UNO to become a prominent figure in Latino/a politics in the city by winning an aldermanic seat, the organization had shifted its interests in developing a Latino/a leadership class. Throughout the hunger strike to the building of the high school, tensions between members of the IPO and UNO would resurrect under the UNO leadership of Juan Rangel.

Hunger Strike as Political and Ideological Opposition to "Business as Usual"

At the time of the hunger strike, La Villita was one of the youngest communities in the city, with 4,000 children of high school age and one public high school with a capacity for 1,800 students (Nambo 2004, 5). Twenty-five percent of the residents had incomes below $15,000. Only 17 percent of all residents had a high school diploma, and 5.5 percent had college degrees. Adding to the concerns was the fact that the overcrowded high school (Farragut Academy) had a 55 percent graduation rate and a dropout rate of 17 percent (ibid.). Forty-two percent of North Lawndale's population lived below the poverty line with a median family income of $18,000. Families with children under eighteen represented 52 percent of the total population under the poverty line, while families with children under five years of age represented 56 percent of the total population. Additionally, the 2000 census reported that 58 percent of families with one or more child under eighteen indicated a grandparent as caregiver (2). In terms of school performance of K–12 students in North Lawndale, 18.6 percent of high school students were performing at or above the state standard. The high school graduation rate in the community was 26.2 percent, with only 3 percent of its residents earning a bachelor's degree (6).

As Jesus Garcia transitioned to become director of LVCDC, residents of the Little Village community, through political and grassroots organizing by way of block club organizations, continued pressure on the city for basic services. Included in this foray was education, as schools in La Villita were chronically overcrowded. Particularly at the high school level, where there was only one school (Farragut Academy) that served students from the neighborhood. In an attempt to further secure the Latino/a vote in La Villita during the mayoral campaign of 1997, local alderman Ricardo Munoz, through support of the mayor's office secured $30 million through the state of Illinois to build a high school in Little Village along with two other high schools in the city (Cortez 2008, 18). Despite Mayor Daley's designating of a site for the school and holding a press conference on the corner of Thirty-First and Kostner as part of his mayoral campaign in 1997, no construction in La Villita took place from 1998 to 2001. Instead, the city of Chicago moved forward with a plan to build two schools from the ground up while refurbishing two others, all four being selective-enrollment high schools. Three of the four schools were scheduled to be built/developed in gentrifying and affluent areas of the city.

When selective enrollment high schools were given first priority, plans to build the high school in La Villita were placed on the back burner. Community members, with the assistance of elected officials for the neighborhood, sought to address the problem through CPS protocols. Outraged at the decision to build the selective enrollment schools, La Villita residents approached CPS. They were given the response that the funds originally allocated to build their high school had been spent. Echoing the sentiments of Kozol, CPS understands the selective enrollment system as

> highly attractive to the more sophisticated parent, disproportionately white and middle class, who have the ingenuity and, now and then, political connections to obtain admission for their children. It is also viewed by some of its defenders as an ideal way to hold while people in the public schools by offering them "choices" that resemble what they'd find in private education. (Kozol 1991, 59–60)

Selective-enrollment schools, created to attract high-achieving students, require applicants to have a particular composite test score upon entry. Prospective applicants are not allowed to take the entrance exam if they do not have the required composite score. These institutions are important politically and physically to a city like Chicago, whose revitalization efforts in housing, commerce, and education are geared toward attracting middle-class residents from the suburbs back into the city. Schools, as the primary conduit in attracting middle-class and affluent residents to a neighborhood, are critical to the city's effort to establish itself as a global city, free of blight and despair. Although viewed positively by many, others, like the residents of North Lawndale and La Villita, understand these new developments as part of a larger effort to displace poor and working-class African-American and Latino/a residents. The process is important to note as many African-American and Latino/a neighborhoods are witnessing the damaging effects of gentrification in the name of "development." Such instances shed light on a process that places the issues and concerns of community members in neighborhoods that have been historically excluded, ignored on the proverbial back-burner when it comes to addressing authentic need.

In the case of Little Village, because the funds were nonrenewable, high school construction was postponed indefinitely. From the indefinite postponement, community members in Little Village were subsequently informed that CPS had come to a final decision not to build a high school. Fortunately, community members refused to take the CPS decision lying down. Recognizing the community's desire to attain a school, community organizer and Little Village resident Tomas Gaete, as employee of the Little Village Community Development Corporation (LVCDC), began to gather community opinions block by block. Because Little Village has a highly organized network of block club associations, Mr. Gaete was able to field the opinions of community members on what should be done to protest CPS and the building of the school. From the concerns of community members fielded by Mr. Gaete, Little Village residents took it upon themselves to attend a leadership training institute organized by LVCDC. In these workshops community members were trained on the basics of community organizing and effective strategies to achieve goals.

After the trainings, community members decided one of their first targets for action would be the CPS board meetings. One of the first approaches was to register for the speaker's list at each board meeting and to express their displeasure at not getting their school. When these tactics didn't yield results, more aggressive approaches were employed. One action even brought a Mariachi band to the board member to sing a song about the high school that was promised to Little Village. In addition, a sit-in was staged in CPS headquarters. Despite the determination of the community in presenting public disgust at CPS's decision, Little Village still did not have a second high school. Upon regrouping, members of the Little Village community decided to take drastic measures. The decision was to stage a hunger strike, beginning on May 13, 2001, ending on June 2 of the same year. This form of protest was chosen due to its ability to demonstrate the seriousness of the community. On the contrary, it was not a decision couched in desperation. Instead, it was an intensely planned strategy to alert CPS of the community's ability to organize and amass power. The hunger strike took place on the site originally planned for the school. Renamed "Camp Cesar Chavez" after the leader of the United Farm Workers, medical staff remained on site in case of emergency. Because some of the hunger strikers were senior citizens, careful attention was given to the hunger strikers as the days progressed. Although there were only fourteen hunger strikers that lasted the nineteen days, community support surpassed the participants' expectation. During the nineteen days the community staged theater events, rallies, and prayer vigils. All were key in keeping the hunger strikers in good spirits.

Of the fourteen *huelgistas* who went the nineteen days, two were under the age of twenty. One was a high school senior at the time (Andrea Guzman), while another is a local community organizer (Samuel "Sammy"

Garcia). Two are grandparents (Manuelita Garcia and Carolina Perez), one I went to college with as an undergraduate (Patricia "Patty" Buenrostro). I was introduced to the protest by a longtime community organizer, also a *huelgista* (Carolina Gaete), who introduced me to her sister, brother, and father, all whom were central to the initiative of the hunger strike (Gema, Claudio, and Tomas Gaete). Recognizing the importance of everyday community members and young people to the development of the community-led initiative, it was agreed by the hunger strikers that all events following the hunger strike in the planning of the school would include the community at large. Within this time period the hunger strikers forced CPS to the negotiating table, resulting in the approval of the high school originally set for construction in 1998. The victory was monumental in that it serves as a living example of the power of communities to organize and mobilize themselves—and produce tangible results.

Simultaneously, in their push for community education, UNO made it known that they wanted a grade school built in the community to address overcrowding. In order to appease both sets of constituents, Alderman Munoz supported a plan to build two schools at the site. UNO, under the leadership of Juan Rangel protested this move, insinuating that gang members would recruit younger students, making both schools a gang stronghold. More political gamesmanship than anything, this move was thought to be retaliation for Munoz's victory in an aldermanic election over a UNO-backed candidate (Cortez 2008, 23).Once the issue was settled that only a high school would be built, CEO Paul Vallas was brought to the Camp Chavez site, and three demands were agreed on orally.

1. The high school will in fact be located at the Thirty-First and Kostner site.

2. That an extraordinary process of community participation for the planning and design of the school and its campus begin immediately. That the strikers prepare and implement this place for a community process that is inclusive and democratic and includes representation from feeder schools.

3. That site preparation will begin within two weeks in order to demonstrate that a good-faith effort is being made toward the construction of the new high school (Cortez, 25).

Despite the oral agreement, there were significant delays to get a written, solidified agreement to build the school. Further complicating matters was the fact that board president Gary Chico left his post to supposedly be with his family. A few days later, Paul Vallas left to pursue a campaign to run for governor. Soon replaced by Arne Duncan as CEO, North Lawndale resident Michael Scott was named as new board president. Under Duncan and Scott, an agreement was made, allocating funds to the building of the school.

As the process moved forward, CPS took hold of much of the process. Contrary to the oral agreements made in the days of the hunger strike, CPS decided they would only engage LVCDC for the planning. This angered members of the hunger strikers, as the community element appeared to be instantly diminished as an "official" process gained momentum. These moments were revisited throughout the planning process, as new people (like myself) were brought into the process, as fewer voices from the hunger strike were present. Discussed in detail in future chapters, these tensions were constant as the days moved closer to the school's opening in 2005.

Adding yet another layer to the progression toward opening day, CPS informed the original planning committee for the high school that African-American residents from the neighboring community of North Lawndale would have to be included in the process. This posed a challenge in that they were brought into the process after the initial organizing by community members in Little Village. As the force of the hunger strike originated in Little Village, African-American residents of North Lawndale were included in the school formation process by CPS's interpretation of a consent decree to desegregate. Operating under the decree since 1981, CPS has been required by the federal government to engage in a concerted effort to desegregate its public schools. Critical to the decree, however, is the idea that desegregation initially implied the inclusion of students of color in "White" schools. The fact that there aren't enough White students in CPS to "desegregate" in this mode has created a process whereby CPS is allowed to interpret what constitutes compliance with the decree. In the attempt to operate in compliance with the mandate, CPS interprets "desegregation" as integrating the four high schools with the neighboring African-American community of North Lawndale. Under the consent decree, each high school is required to maintain a population that is no less than 30 percent African-American and no more that 70 percent Latino/a. As a loose interpretation of the desegregation mandate, CPS is able to argue to the federal government that their attempts at new school development remain in concert with the legal statute. Throughout the design team process this became an issue as many parents and community members in North Lawndale knew little about the strike, and initially felt as if they were being "tokenized" for the sole purpose of acting in compliance with a federal mandate.

Currently the building houses four schools: (1) multicultural academic scholarship (originally multicultural arts—MAS); (2) school of math, science, and technology (Infinity); (3) world languages; and (4) SOJO. The "school-within-a-school" concept was a design chosen by members of the community to provide students with the ability to choose their educational paths. Since opening day on September 6, 2005, the school has opened with four hundred students (one hundred freshmen in each high school). Each school received one hundred more students in fall semesters of 2006, 2007, and 2008, totaling 1,600 students for the entire multiplex (400 students per school). Remembering the spirit of the hunger strike, the original planning committee vowed that the new high school complex would be a space that reflected the core values of democracy, community ownership, self-discipline, flexibility, collaboration, lifelong learning, innovation, accountability, leadership development, cross-cultural respect, efficacy, teamwork, and empowerment. The core values were key in the inclusion of the African-American community, as students from two distinct ethnicities and cultural backgrounds converge on one cite in a hyper-segregated city.

In recognizing the historical colonial relationship between communities and universities, I entered the process understanding that my work would be impossible without the community's blessing. I agree that "it is not ethical to walk away, or simply to carry out projects which describe what is already known" (Thuwai Smith 2012, 140). In this sense the roles and relationships go beyond the ethics of traditional qualitative research and involve transparency with the people I work with who are not university professors.

Understanding the permanent, engrained, and enduring properties of racism posed many challenges for the design team. While some members in both groups were reluctant at first, there were some who took the issue head-on. They reminded the group of the collective struggle of Black and Latino/a peoples and how White supremacy (racism) has functioned in the past to divide and conquer, resulting in distrust and self-segregation. Coupled with the historical legacy of CPS and its treatment of low-income working-class Black and Latino/a youth, we continually found ourselves at a crossroads when it came between choosing accountability to the community initiative and compliance with CPS policy. It became especially difficult when the people responsible for communicating CPS policy and mandates to the design team in many cases were African-American and Latino/a. Even more troubling was the fact that many understood how hegemonic bureaucracies derail community initiatives. On numerous occasions we were "advised" on how not to "ruffle the feathers" of CPS in creating the high school. In the liberal sense, they felt that they were "doing us a favor." In reality, it often felt like they were agents of the state with the sole intent of defeating the goal of having the school come to fruition.

Chapter 2

To Create a School

Uneasy Partnerships with the Central Office

In light of the developments that brought the school to fruition, this chapter describes the processes engaged in immediately after the hunger strike, moving toward the development of the design teams and the Transition Advisory Council (TAC). From the initial conversations with Chicago Public Schools to the building of the physical school building, the process maintained a series of ebbs and flows. As the theme of contestation permeates much of the process of developing the school, the struggle to maintain the principles emanating from the hunger strike presented numerous challenges at the level of the design teams and in the TAC. Because the process stems from a community-based initiative, the ascribed values of the community fostered during and after the hunger strike did not translate well to the neoliberal, bureaucratic, procedures of CPS. Highlighting the contested negotiations between community residents and CPS, the chapter uses counterstory from a cross-section of participants in the various formations that were developed immediately after the hunger strike. In this instance counterstory operates in Yosso and Solorzano's version of a practice that is reflective of the data gathered from the research, existing literature, and personal and professional experiences coupled with collective and community memory (Yosso and Solorzano 2005, 125). Where it is impossible to confirm the intentions of individuals inside the CPS bureaucracy, as an active appendage of the neoliberal state, their presence, policies, and actions of the central office were constantly understood as broad-based attempts to curtail authentic community engagement.

Additionally, the remainder of the chapter does not lend itself to a chronological account of events. Instead, due of the overlapping nature of the affairs in question, they are discussed in relationship to each other, with the understanding that there were few explicit instances where one group ended and another began. Despite working under particular CPS deadlines, the names of the committees remained fluid for a time, due to the dynamic between community stakeholders and the central office. As the names of the formations changed, sentiments sometime shifted with the adjustments and reconfigurations, depending on the event and the particular group. Its relation to SOJO represents the necessary precursors to provide a glimpse into the messiness of layered and contested space relative to community intent, researcher collaboration, partisan politics, and the central office bureaucracy.

From Promise to Vision

The days directly after the hunger strike, like much of the process to get to opening day, were a murky collection of overlapping events as I became officially involved almost a year later. Over the years, with the assistance of documentation from numerous sources coupled with my conversations with people who were directly involved provided clarity on the nature of events moving forward from the hunger strike. Because the CPS narrative reluctantly mentions the hunger strike as merely an "event," the counter-stories of those involved provide a grounded account of the struggles and interaction with state power. From their counternarratives the theme of contestation is realized.

Directly following the hunger strike there were a series of three town hall meetings held in La Villita to plot the direction of the school's creation. Facilitated by LVCDC, a series of committees were developed to plot the direction of the future work. Hereafter referenced as the "three original committees," they were curriculum, community programs, and facilities design. I was most familiar with curriculum and community programs, as the architecture plans had just been completed when I entered the process. Directly following the town hall meetings and the development of the original committees, a list of recommendations were delivered to CPS as to what should be included in the school. In addition to the $5 million secured from the board to purchase the land, members of the curriculum meeting collected over three hundred surveys in the neighborhood. To paraphrase the original question asked of community members, the language included a question to the order of "If you could close your eyes and you could send your kid to the most beautiful ideal school that you could imagine, what would that school look like?" (Martinez interview, July 9, 2012). Five central themes came back from the surveys: (1) schools where our children are known as human beings, (2) high levels of personalization, (3) high levels of trusting adult-child relationships, (4) a place where young people are safe, and (5) a place where young people are supported (ibid.). Because the community victory came about at the height of the small schools movement, the curriculum took those needs and interpreted them into content. In order to realize schools that encompassed the themes from the surveys, the curriculum committee felt it was best encapsulated in a school that focused on language as a critical component of identity. The second foci would be a school that focused on the visual and performing arts as a critical component of identity. Third was a school that focused on math, science, and technology. Last, to commemorate the core values of the hunger strike of equity, cooperative power, gender equity, justice, and access came the social justice theme (ibid.). From these surveys, the world language, multicultural arts, math, science and technology, and social justice high schools were born.

During this progression CPS made numerous attempts to insert itself as primary actor in the process of developing the school. Although not without intense contestation, community members on the Advisory Board and its subsequent iteration as the TAC were clear on maintaining the values developed during the hunger strike, despite CPS's advances. These moments were revisited throughout the planning process, as new people (like myself) were brought into the fold, as a contingency of *huelgistas* and community members held CPS and others in the new configurations accountable to the values of the hunger strike.

Kitchen Table Meeting

After the hunger strike and after going to the campsite, my involvement came by way of a request from Carolina (Caro) Gaete (one of the *huelgistas*) and Jose Rico (who would later become principal at the MAS high school). They wanted to talk to people they knew about the responsibility that had been placed on them as a community. It was held at Caro's house, and centered around a conversation about the possibilities for a school that's starting from scratch as a result of a community-driven effort. As someone who was originally alerted of the hunger strike by Caro, I appreciated that she followed up with me and thought of me as someone who could engage the huelgistas and LVCDC about next steps. For myself, it was an exciting time, in that this was the rare opportunity to build a CPS school from the ground up. At the meeting's close, Caro and Rico informed me that they would be in contact with me at a later date.

Simultaneously my excitement was paired with a personal struggle centered in the "problem" of academics engaging themselves in community-based initiatives. Just as I was excited about the potential to build a school with people I know and respect, I also thought it might not have been the best idea to bring me to the table. Holding the occupation as university professor and researcher is difficult for me at times, understanding the historical exploitative relationship between research universities and communities. In previous experiences I have been in the presence of other academics who are wrongly positioned as the "expert" in relation to a community's struggle for justice in vital areas (i.e., food security, housing, education, etc.). Where I am most familiar with these instances in educational settings, I have always subscribed to the school of thought that trepidation and skepticism by community members is a good thing. After numerous experiences of witnessing the paternalistic practice of demeaning and dehumanizing communities, I quickly became aware of the things I did not want to do. However, beyond my academic credentials, I am still a concerned resident of Chicago, who is invested in the future of public education. By remaining accountable to the initial community struggle, pairing the contestation of both spaces (researcher and Chicago resident) presents real challenges.

Luckily, my experiences with community-engaged research have also afforded me the opportunity to read and work with those who have engaged in the work with humility and solidarity. The scholarship and actions of Lipman, Tuhiwai Smith, Duncan-Andrade, Fine, Cammarota, Camangian, and Pulido ring loudly in their reminders of the dangers of research without accountability. If I was to be contacted by the group again, I knew that it would be critically important to operate from within a space of humility. I was reminded by people I respect that I was not called to the table solely for my skill set as a researcher, but for who the community members know me to be. Above all else, this was critical as we moved forward with the process of developing the school.

Rounding out my challenges was the fact that as a potential participant I would be an African-American male in a hypersegregated city working with a community struggle driven by Latino/a residents. Where there wasn't any personal trepidation, I also wanted to prepare myself for the potential political and social tensions that could arise due to my involvement. Though there were brief moments of harmony during the Harold Washington mayoral administration (1983–1987), these moments were fleeting in a city deeply rooted in unilateral mayoral administrations. Rooted in over a century of patronage and quid pro quo deals, neighborhoods and ethnic groups are in perpetually pitted against each other for resources distributed by the mayor. As payment for these resources, the constituencies must demonstrate their allegiance to the mayor by way of votes and support for his policies in matters of education, employment, housing, and commerce. Even though the twenty-second ward (where La Villita is housed), has a history of staunch independence from machine politics, it was hard to assess who possible detractors (if any) would be. At the time, these were my initial thoughts. I still hadn't been invited back to work with the group.

Layers of Community Engagement from La Villita and North Lawndale

The following section provides a discussion on the cross-section of people who informed my ability to understand the layers of events directly following the community victory. From my interactions with them over the years in numerous capacities, their counterstories, along with others, were integral to my participation in the process. Because research and praxis do not have a seamless relationship, explicit efforts to humanize our work are critical. By providing counterstory to contest the dominant deficit-based narrative on low-income/working-class communities of color, the voices of those intimate to the process become the grounded voice of expertise. As we moved toward the specific development of SOJO on the design team, the larger process involving the TAC affords a space in which to engage subtle victories and heated conflict. These layers shed light on the processes of formation of the school, paired with the challenges of living in a hyper-segregated, politically charged environment.

Soon after the kitchen table meeting, I remember meeting Rito Martinez (SOJO's first principal) at a house party in La Villita. We talked briefly on a couch about his work with the curriculum committee formed by the *huelgistas* and the work he was currently doing at Morton East as a history teacher. I didn't think of it then, but this was the start of a series of relationships that endured the design team process into opening day and with the first group of students that matriculated through SOJO. In the beginning there was an air of excitement, but we would soon find out that the initial excitement of a community-driven victory is often met with the harsh reality that is the central office politics in Chicago.

Because Rito grew up in the neighborhood, he became familiar with the movement through struggle on the way to his mother's house.

I was comin' home to my mom's after Morton East, after school let out and I was with my girl who was an organizer in Cicero. I was driving over the bridge and I saw the hunger strike. So I pull over and I knew half the people there. That's where I grew up. So at that moment I knew this is where I need to be. And so I supported the last couple of days of the hunger strike and just got involved full time. Met Caro, met Claudio. I had already known Jaime, Chuy, all the other folks, 'cus that's where I grew up . . . I was going home to see my mom. (Interview, July 9, 2012)

Rito's initial involvement allowed me to understand some of the layers of the events after the strike. After the three town hall meetings that were held directly after the strike, Rito witnessed the development of the original three committees (curriculum, community programs, and facilities design) that would soon morph into the design teams and the TAC. Along with a host of others, his infusion to the process of developing the school directly after the strike is integral to providing an account that runs counter to CPS's recollection of the hunger strike.

Another person who was critical to my understanding of the events moving to the formation of the various committees was Cynthia Nambo. As we were undergraduates together at a local state university, I had become familiar with her activism as an award-winning classroom teacher and community advocate for public education. Knowing her work, she was a welcome addition to the process throughout my time on the design team. Her work in the areas of school development and instructional level remains invaluable. Discussed in detail in later sections, her development of the proposal process and protocols allowed for community concerns to be prioritized in the creation of the school.

Jaime De Leon was an employee of LVCDC at the time of the hunger strike. His efforts to organize and garner support for the high school along with other employees at LVCDC were instrumental in making sure the community remained central in the process of the developing the school. His involvement from the hunger strike to opening day allowed for consistency and coordination in numerous formations of the group.

Tiffany Childress was an implant to Chicago by way of a community-based program she worked in as an undergraduate. As a bilingual African-American woman, her efforts were crucial in garnering support from both North Lawndale and La Villita. From working in La Villita originally and coming to live in North Lawndale, she came to the conclusion that "if I was going to affect poverty in North Lawndale and Little Village, I would have to impact schools" (interview, July 31, 2012). Her discussion of her process of navigating the tensions between both communities moving toward opening day were of maximum importance as we moved toward opening day. Having the challenging task of speaking between both communities placed her in the middle of racial, political, and social turmoil throughout the process.

Directly following the strike, Carmen Mahon was a community activist and school counselor who worked with schools in North Lawndale. In the early stages of her community involvement, I knew Carmen as an undergraduate student from the South Side of the city pushing for authentic community engagement from the university she was attending. True to her word, she continued working with schools and community members on Chicago's West Side. She was brought into the process by way of her employment at the Umoja Student Development Corporation (originating at Manley High School) and from her numerous connections from Lawndale Christian Church and its organizing wing of the Lawndale Community Development Corporation (LCDC). Her ability to ask critical questions from a community perspective became important as the work moved forward.

Aquil Charlton was a founding member of a community organization called the Crib Collective. Because of its geographic location (it was near Ogden Avenue, one of the unspoken boarder streets between La Villita and North Lawndale), the collective made numerous attempts to engage youth from North Lawndale and Little Village. This was critical, as members from both communities pushed for youth involvement with the process. As an organization rooted in social entrepreneurship, its communal process was instrumental in providing perspectives from youth from both communities. More than a novel idea, the existence of the Crib Collective as a multiracial organization in a hypersegregated city provided an important example of possibility for members of the design team and the TAC. I had become aware of the Crib Collective's work around the same time as the strike, when Aquil worked as an Americorps leader in a Public Allies regional office in Chicago.

Josephine (Josie) Yanguas and Linda Corronado were vocal members of the TAC. Predating the hunger strike, both had experiences as members of the Independent Political Organization (IPO) of the twenty-second ward. Their involvement was critical as two people who were familiar not only with schools by way of experience (Linda as a member of the school board and as a classroom teacher and counselor; Josie's as employee of an organization specifically designed to locate resources for local schools; both are also members of local school councils). Their ability to recognize the political tensions while also recognizing what schools need to function were critical additions.

In the attempt to locate my involvement, these were the people who were able to ground my understanding of the order of events that ensued directly after the victory was achieved. Some I met during the process of developing the school (Rito, Jaime, Josie, Linda, and Tiffany), while others I've known from working in the city with community organizations and schools (Cynthia, Carmen, Aquil). As discussed in detail in the next section, I became deeply acquainted with a host of new and existing relationships that would last during and beyond the process.

First Interaction with the Large Group

As the months passed after my kitchen table meeting, I hadn't heard from the group I met with. At the same time, it had come to my attention that there was some level of formation and the groups were in the process of their initial meetings and had begun to move toward creating the school. Shortly after hearing this, I received an e-mail from Mike Klonsky, one of the founders of the Small Schools Workshop, inviting me to a work session in Little Village connected to the hunger strike. Championed by himself, Sue Klonsky, and Bill Ayers, the Small Schools Workshop in Chicago was instrumental in sparking a national dialogue in the mid-1990s to create smaller school structures and "small learning communities" (SLCs). The purpose was to create situations in which students could receive more on-one-on instruction, in addition to teachers having more opportunities to create curriculum with each other across content areas (Klonsky and Klonsky 2012). The small schools movement gained considerable notoriety as schools across the country were moving in this direction with measureable results. Before Mike's e-mail, the three committees were meeting, deciding on the various community programs and the design of the school. The meeting he invited me to took place at LVCDC's office on Twenty-Ninth and Harding.

When I first sat down I noticed there were architectural design plans on one of the wall of the office space, as members of the facilities com- mittee met to decide on the physical external and internal design of the building. Being at the height of the small schools movement, the curriculum committee made the decision to go with the small schools model to best ensure that students would have access to quality instruction. In addition to those who were working through their connection to LVCDC, I also made my first contact with numerous members of philanthropists organizations that provided funds to support the work—the National Council of La Raza (NCLR), the Chicago High Schools Redesign Initiative (CHSRI), the Chicago Community Trust (CCT), and CPS's Office of New Schools (ONS). In addition to the advocacy and philanthropic organizations with representatives in attendance, I was also alerted to the fact that other grant-awarding organizations had jumped on with the Gates Foundation and the Chicago Community Trust through CHSRI to provide funding for the initiative (one of the philanthropic organizations that provided funds in the early stages was the Polk Bros. Foundation). Despite my personal disdain for many philanthropic organizations that operate in low-income/working-class communities of color, further strengthening the Nonprofit Industrial Complex (Incite! 2006) we did find a trusted ally in the Chicago Community Trust and the CHSRI by way of Patricia (Pat) Ford. She was instrumental in securing initial funds to support some of the innovations in the first years of the school. Also present at the meeting was Cynthia Nambo, who was a welcome sight due to my knowledge of her work in previous instances.

To bring national advocacy organizations to the table, members of LVCDC used their connections through Jaime De Leon (a former NCLR employee) to take notice of the community victory in La Villita. Once they learned about the community victory they pledged support by way of a $500,000 grant for technical support, professional development, and what was then expansion of their early college initiative. This initiative created programming in schools that would enroll high school students in college courses as early as their junior year, providing them with early entrance credit upon graduation from high school. From the outset, the world language high school was targeted for the early college program. However, funds initially intended to be solely for world language were spread for technical assistance for all four school.

In this particular iteration, because there was no TAC or design team in place, the meeting was an amalgamation of members from the three original committees. At this point there wasn't an "official" name for this configuration, but this could be considered one of the gatherings that planted the seeds for the groupings that would guide the process into opening day. At this point there was no discussion of the involvement of North Lawndale, but these conversations were soon to come.

From "Board in Formation" to the TAC

Overlapping with the attendance boundaries/consent decree issue was the logistical and tactile formation of the design team and the Transition Advisory Council (TAC). Once funding was secured from the various philanthropic and advocacy groups in addition to the central office, Cynthia Nambo was contracted as a consultant to solidify and design the process to develop the organizational capacity of the four schools. Like the majority of people who were instrumental to the process, she started off as a volunteer and was brought on due to her adept skill in capacity development, school culture, and curriculum alignment. From my observations and experiences with her, as a person who was intent on building capacity as we moved toward becoming design teams and the TAC, she was a trusted member of the process. Though the hunger strike was a colossal victory in terms of getting the school built, the other part of the equation included developing processes and practices to develop the day-to-day operations of a school. Often after such a powerful community victory, the day-to-day operations needed to remain accountable to the community-driven effort are overlooked. Due to the technical capacities needed to effectively run a school, a trusted collaborator is needed.

Especially in a tension-filled situation like this, where the central office is resentful of the victory and is reluctant to provide the community with all things necessary to develop effective schools. Armed with a theoretical and practical knowledge of school culture, staff development, curriculum implementation, and instructional support, Cynthia's work with various individuals and community entities was critical to our process.

By placing community concerns in the center, her design of numerous protocols and practices remained central to the development of the final request for proposals (RFP). The fact that Cynthia was the primary author of the "CHSRI New Schools Starts Grant RFP for Creating Small Chicago Public High Schools at the Little Village Campus" (Chicago High School Redesign Initiative 2004) was critical to our process. Because this was the document that CPS approved to be used by the TAC to evaluate the proposals, it ensured that each of the design teams had to explicitly demonstrate how the values developed during the hunger strike would be represented in their respective school. To have this at the proposal stage was powerful. By controlling the language of the RFP and getting CPS to approve it, members of the various groups entrusted to bring the school to fruition were able to develop their respective schools as institutions centered in community concerns.

At this point the messiness came by way of the revolving door of CPS policy. Due to the new infusion of Gates Foundation funding by way of CHSRI, CPS created a process modeled after the original committee structure without giving them credit. Because CPS's Office of New Schools (ONS) decided to provide access to CHSRI funds, they felt as if it was in their purview to dictate the process of creating a TAC. Because there was already a group in formation, it made it difficult for CPS to impose its will.

For these reasons, this was not a smooth or sanguine process. For the remainder of the progression to opening day, CPS maintained its status as adversarial partner. Maintaining the values of the hunger strike proved difficult as the work moved forward. After the three committees were formed and the $5 million was secured from the board for the purchase of the land, the responsibility quickly shifted to make sure that the community process was maintained. The work of members of the original committees fueled the future work, keeping CPS at bay when they made the attempt to influence the work. As a skilled tactician, Cynthia was able to work with the existing group of members from the original committees and other community partners recruited by LVCDC to ensure the centrality of community concerns. At this moment, one of the representatives from NCLR sent to work with Cynthia would refer to the group as a "board in formation." I recall numerous meetings with group members from La Villita and North Lawndale in numerous spaces throughout both neighborhoods for capacity development workshops run by Cynthia and various consultants brought into the process. Soon after, the same group was referenced as the Little Village High School Advisory Board (taken from the folder issued to members of the Advisory board). Once CPS became involved through the Office of New Schools (ONS), they brought the name Transition Advisory Council (TAC) to the committee. The group as the TAC would be responsible for reviewing proposals from design teams that desired a space in the school. The name was still strange in that there were existing workings in place where members of both neighborhoods were already organized by LVCDC and LCDC before the name change. Once CPS came with the claim that the TAC was a requirement for any new school approved by ONS, the group was pressed to comply with the CPS mandate. Once the group was officially recognized as a TAC, they began to bring other community members to the fold. Along with myself and Rito, we were part of the first design team specifically for SOJO. We were responsible for recruiting families, concerned community members, and teachers to our design team to develop the RFP to be submitted to the TAC. The TAC included an interview process that would vet potential members on their knowledge of both communities, education, and their willingness to work as a collective. Discussed in detail in the next section, members of North Lawndale were included on the advisory committee, as students from North Lawndale were needed to attend the four schools in compliance with a federal consent decree to desegregate. The inclusion of North Lawndale was contested, and has remained a contentious issue.

Because there was a bevy of new schools that were applying for CHSRI funds, CPS's version of the TAC now required community groups to have the public officials on the committee, ensuring that local politicians remained abreast of the issues. The city council member from La Villita was on call for the TAC, as he was trained by IPO organizers and was the former chief of Staff for the executive director of LVCDC when he was a local alderman. The same could not be said for the local alderman representing North Lawndale, as he rarely attended any of the TAC meetings.

Members of the earlier formation remember interviewing each other for the TAC to ensure that the community values were upheld. In the end, the original TAC had twenty members, primarily from La Villita. Despite funding from CHSRI and CPS's Office of New Schools, Cynthia developed the RFP that each design team was required to submit. When she was originally brought into the process by LVCDC, she thought that she would only be working to develop the World Language high school by way of the NCLR funding. As her time on the design teams progressed, NCLR, CHSRI, and CPS became the main funding entities for the work.

For the design team, the newly formed TAC was already in the process of maintaining a closed process for the approval of the design teams. Originally CPS wanted to make a citywide RFP for design teams that desired a school in the multiplex building. The community was able to avert this by making sure that CPS knew that if RFPs were accepted from those who were unfamiliar with the community struggle, it would make it more difficult to uphold the values. Because the values were written in the RFP, the TAC could make the argument that the wording of the RFP spoke to the need to a group that was familiar with the hunger strike and had intimate knowledge of both communities. The unusual instance of making sure that there was representation of North Lawndale in the process also lent itself to keeping the RFP closed to the larger city while centering on both neighborhoods. This was evident through Cynthia's ability to create protocols that perpetually demonstrated to CPS that the TAC and its community partners were consistent in their actions.

> The issue here is not about fighting . . . it's about follow-through . . . and that's your fight. Because if you follow-through, then all you do is have evidence that's compelling and nobody can push it . . . but that community piece right there is so important and having meetings with multiple stakeholders that are effective and have impact and not just technical and it happened and you check it off a list . . . but our meetings were productive. If I didn't design it . . . If I didn't have my evidence and my e-mails and if I didn't have my . . . if I didn't get to the TAC or the advisory committee and really didn't have them understand what we were doing and make the decisions along the way so when we had to meet with CPS . . . *Boom!* . . . we were strong . . . we were strong and they saw that . . . they saw that every meeting . . . (Cynthia Nambo interview, June 2012)

Critical to her development in the beginning was technical support from NCLR. By way of the coaches they employed to assist Cynthia, she spoke about how critical they were to her development. On one occasion I had a chance to meet one of the NCLR coaches, Peter Burmudes, who worked closely with Cynthia to develop protocols for the TAC and design team. I remember specifically being impressed with his knowledge of schools and the ways in which to make them accessible to communities.

In addition to her work rewriting the CHSRI proposal, I remember attending a number of Praxis Institutes she developed (weekend-long workshops/retreats to develop team capacity), to get design team members prepared to write the RFP while becoming acquainted with all of the processes necessary to have a functioning school. Unfortunately, like many things imbued in the NPIC, she had to leave the work as a paid consultant because the funding for her position ran out before we could implement the entirety of protocols she created. However, her work remained critical to our development.

CPS Interpretations of Desegregation and a Consent Decree

Adding yet another layer to the progression toward opening day, soon after the school was approved, CPS informed the original planning committee that African-American residents from the neighboring community of North Lawndale would have to be included in the process. This process would revisit itself in the ensuing years, but it was also an issue as neighborhood high schools get their students by way of creating an attendance boundary. This posed a challenge in that they were brought into the process after the initial organizing by community members in Little Village. Before the design teams and TAC were officially recognized, the attendance boundaries were an issue throughout the development of the school and well after the schools opened their doors. Plugged as a political wedge issue, local elected officials saw education as the matter that provided them the greatest opportunity to secure support and future votes. In a what-have-you-done-for-me-lately city like Chicago, an issue like the inclusion of African-American residents and attendance boundaries fit perfectly into the age-old colonial practice of divide and conquer. As a de facto function of White supremacy, the idea of having two communities pitted against each other allowed CPS to engage in the process of making it difficult for communities to realize points of unity. Despite the adjacent locales of both communities, regional segregation disallowed the process of engagement and dialogue. After a watershed event like the hunger strike, it was difficult to convince some residents of La Villita that their school should be shared with neighbors next door. Because conflicting histories and fear of neighborhood violence (both communities have a documented history of gang violence) were real and not just perceived for some, the added layer of stereotype rooted in unfamiliarity created a formidable barrier for active participants in the school's formation.

For residents of North Lawndale, this tension was never resolved as residents remained skeptical about their inclusion in the process. As the hunger strike originated in Little Village, African-American residents of North Lawndale were included in the school-formation process by CPS's interpretation of a consent decree to desegregate, not as a community considered to be a target of the initiative, despite sharing two existing schools that serve both communities (Corkery Elementary and Farragut Academy). Operating under the decree since 1981 (and recently rescinded by the federal courts in 2009), CPS has been required by the federal government to engage in a concerted effort to desegregate its public schools. Critical to the decree however, is the idea that desegregation initially implied the inclusion of students of color in "White" schools. The fact that there aren't enough White students in CPS to "desegregate" in this mode has created a process where CPS is allowed to interpret what constitutes compliance with the decree. In the attempt to operate in compliance with the mandate, CPS interprets "desegregation" as integrating the four high schools with the neighboring African-American community of North Lawndale. Under CPS's interpretation of the consent decree, the Lawndale Little Village Multiplex was required to maintain a population that was no less than 30 percent African-American and no more that 70 percent Latino/a. As a loose interpretation of the desegregation mandate, CPS is able to argue to the federal government that their attempts at new school development remain in concert with the legal statute. Throughout the design team process this became an issue, as many parents and community members in North Lawndale knew little about the strike, and initially felt as if they were being "tokenized" for the sole purpose of acting in compliance with a federal mandate.

Further complicating matters was the fact that CPS used their in-house demographer to arbitrarily create a boundary plan that would get the closest to ensuring a school population that was 30 percent African-American and 70 percent Latino/a. This upset residents of La Villita due to existing gang (street organization) tensions and the elimination of the eastern end of the neighborhood from the attendance boundary (field notes, February 7, 2005). A similar situation was happening across the city as schools were being closed or phased out. Students from distant neighborhoods would be sent to an arbitrary school that resulted in major problems, largely in the form of violence intertwined between street organization rivalries and tensions between neighborhoods facilitated by regional hypersegregation. If a student has to cross major street organization lines, either on foot or by public transportation, there was the potential for a host of problems. Similar situations were on the minds of parents from both communities as Thirty-First Street, Pulaski, and Kostner were all major thoroughfares that could potentially have young people crossing certain boundaries. Rito's take on the situation was critical as a member of the SOJO design team.

> When the boundaries were drawn at Hamlin and didn't include at least half of LV, there were people that were angry because of two reasons: One because of the desperation for a school choice that was not Farragut . . . people had been desperate for twenty to thirty years for a choice that would meet the needs of their kids across different gang lines/boundaries. Historic plantation politics that the city had created to divide North Lawndale and South Lawndale in such a way where we engender racial tensions as a means of responding to the coalition-making of Lozano and Washington so those systems were in place that people were rooted to in their desperation for school choice. . . . I think that was a battle that was ultimately lost because of the magnitude of the systemic injustices issues perpetrated on the community

historically, and we just could not get away from it. (Martinez interview, July 8, 2012)

While Martinez's commentary sheds light on the deeply entrenched racial understandings in a segregated city, it should be noted that even on the TAC this was a situation met with trepidation. Many of the participants in the process, while aware of the tensions, were not as vocal about the realities the group faced moving forward.

Similar to the role played by Cynthia in the development of the RFP and ensuring that the values of the hunger strike were represented throughout the process, Tiffany Childress was a critical addition to the advisory committee and then the TAC. As a young organizer coming from Ohio, her experiences in Chicago as an undergraduate student informed her practice in the work moving forward. Coupled with her organizational skills, as a bilingual African-American woman she possessed a capacity that few members from North Lawndale possessed: the ability to speak Spanish.

Before I was introduced to Tiffany, I met Stanley Merriwether (then–executive director of LCDC) at the LVCDC office. At a meetings of the advisory committee (pre-TAC) she alerted me that she hired a young organizer originally from Los Angeles who had been living in Ohio. When LVCDC approached LCDC about garnering support for getting residents from North Lawndale, the first person that came to mind was Tiffany Childress. Because she lived in North Lawndale and had experiences working in North Lawndale and La Villita, she would be the perfect person to represent North Lawndale as a member of the TAC with Stanley.

As an undergraduate, she was always fascinated and discouraged by the hypersegregation of Chicago. Coming from Los Angeles and then Ohio, she was unfamiliar with a city that had explicit boundaries where racial groups had little interaction with each other. Nevertheless, when she got word of the inclusion of North Lawndale residents (Tiffany Childress interview, July 31, 2012), she was excited about the opportunity to finally do some peer-to-peer work. When she first came to the TAC she also found the work intimidating.

People in Chicago were trying to make you pick boxes . . . The first few meetings were overwhelming and intimidating. I was a young organizer . . . young in terms of age and experience as an organizer. All of these powerful people in the room. All this lingo . . . the learning curve was steep . . . I had to learn all these acronyms. Chicago is the city of acronyms. That was really

overwhelming for me. Stanley wanted me to be more vocal, but
I like to process things. (ibid.)

However, organizing in North Lawndale was more of a process of
simply "talking to her neighbors." Because she was already known in the
area, it was easier to develop trust among community members. Nevertheless, she noticed great trepidation from North Lawndale residents, due to
the idea that they were unwanted "add-ons" to the process. In her account
of her interaction with a community elder, she reluctantly became aware
of the unspoken politics often present in community-driven initiatives in
Chicago. Soon after writing a column for a local newspaper, she received a
call from a former high school principal.

> I got a call from this gentlemen, the (former) principal of
> Collins, and he basically read me my rights, he just told me
> that we did the same process thirty years ago . . . The city is
> going to do what they're going to do . . . they're just using
> you . . . Mexicans don't really want you there . . . it's a political
> ploy . . . it's a deseg decree . . . this is a principal right? . . . and
> this is an activist principal . . . and I'm young and wet behind
> the ears . . . I didn't know what he was talking about . . . I
> just felt . . . part of me dismissed him as old cynical outdated
> leader . . . you know . . . who had his heyday. And then my
> optimism said this is a new day, we're really trying to work to-
> ward racial conciliation and racial collaboration . . . it was very
> insulting for me . . . but I was raised by my grandparents, so
> at the same time there was this respect for him 'cause he was
> an elder but there was this weird tension . . . should I believe
> him? Am I being stupid? . . . but what he said I think a lot
> of other residents felt that weren't able to articulate in the way
> that a principal could. (ibid.)

Taking into account the permanent, engrained, and enduring properties of racism/White supremacy, the former principal was giving her a historical lesson on the development of Collins High School. It was originally
developed for residents of La Villita and North Lawndale some thirty years
prior, but Mexican-American residents were not interested in traveling east
and north to go to school in the Collins building. Sentiment such as the
ones from the principal, while not the overriding opinion of residents of
North Lawndale, were critical to recognize as the process moved forward.

Contrasting the principal's views, while some members from both communities were reluctant at first, there were some who took the issue head-on. They reminded the group of the collective struggle of Black and Latino/a peoples and how White supremacy/racism has functioned in the past to divide and conquer, resulting in distrust and self-segregation. Simultaneously, some felt as if this represented a genuine effort from some members of the TAC, while it felt like empty rhetoric from others.

Carmen Mahon wrestled with this throughout the process. As a member of the advisory board and then as a member of the TAC, she would also discuss what those tensions meant and how she would come to grips with them during the process. At the time she was working for Umoja Student Development Corporation as a youth counselor. She was also brought into the process by Stanley Merriwether, who knew the executive director of Umoja at the time. The sentiments rode deep with her in that

> There was intention to be genuine. The undertone was still doing things for our own. Wasn't no Black folks on that hunger strike so you know . . . even though we want to bridge the relationship with Black and Brown, South and North, it was this undertone . . . we did this . . . South Lawndale Little Village . . . Mexican Mothers went on a strike so why should they . . . why should Black folks be a part of that? But I think the theme of unity . . . someone kept it threaded in the conversation . . . the genuineness of that was intentional that someone . . . whatever that was . . . but at the end of the day (the community still felt as if) this is ours (Carmen Mahon interview, July 20, 2012)

She also felt that some people involved in the process understood the vision, but the social and political climate between both neighborhoods made it very difficult to penetrate age-old fears rooted in years of having little contact with each other. Rito Martinez shared similar sentiments about the challenges of authentically engaging residents in North Lawndale.

> The other issue was the consent decree that was extremely important . . . and it think it was on CPS intentionality to come on the twelfth hour and let us know that . . . it just seemed desperate. We had to intentionally address the participation of North Lawndale. We engaged folks at the community organization level, but not on the ground level. The first battle had

never considered North Lawndale . . . so how do you engage
someone in a group or when you actually didn't know you were
fighting for them. . . . I think the values of the hunger strike
transcended the inclusive diverse, education of Black and Brown
youth, but it was an afterthought by way of the consent decree.
(Martinez interview, July 9, 2012)

Unfortunately, these tensions lasted throughout the process and continue
to this day.

The Idea of Including Youth

In addition to the boundaries concerns, review of design team proposals
and final recommendations to CPS, the authentic inclusion of young people
became the responsibility of the TAC. In order to secure permanent spaces
for young people in the planning process of the school, the TAC created
the youth advocate position. Responsibilities of the youth advocate included
holding youth council meetings and representing youth positions on the
advisory board. Remaining accountable to both communities, the youth
advocate position was shared by two youth workers from North Lawndale
(Aquil Carlton and Esmeralda "Esme" Baltazar) and a youth worker from
Little Village (Jorge Roque). Aquil and Esme shared the youth advocate
position on the TAC, as they alternated in attendance for TAC meetings.

Aquil and Esme were members of the Crib Collective, a grassroots
organization attempting to model health community practices for young
people of color from North Lawndale and Little Village. Similar to Tiffany's
contribution, the Crib Collective provided a tangible example of young
people making a concerted effort to address the needs of the community by
way of intentional modeling of problem solving. One of the first meetings
I had was in North Lawndale at the Crib Collective headquarters. When
CPS made the announcement that North Lawndale had to be included in
the process, we met to discuss inclusion and potential tensions.

At first glance, the process may appear contradictory to "authentic"
youth participation, but the adults in the position of youth advocate were
grounded in their involvement with youth. In many instances youth initiatives claiming to include the opinions of young people use youths symboli-
cally. Rarely are youth trained to make leadership decisions that determine
the direction of the organization. In the attempt to break from such practices, the youth advocates were making a concerted effort to provide young

people with the necessary leadership development to make informed decisions on policies that will govern the four high schools. The representative
position of youth advocate came about for logistical reasons. In the transition from the advisory committee to the TAC, many of the meetings were
held at night (due to work schedules of TAC members). Because many
of the members of the youth council were aged eleven to fourteen, many
parents were worried about their safety in traveling the neighborhood at
night. To accommodate parental concerns, youth council meetings were held
in the afternoon. The youth advocates of the TAC, in organizing the youth
council meetings, became responsible for report-backs to the advisory board
and the youth council. Stressing authentic participation of young people, it
became crucially important for the youth advocates to operate as liaisons
between the TAC and youth council. Any conflicts between the two groups
in terms of ideology would have to be negotiated by the youth advocates.

For the purposes of the high school, the two adult youth advocates
assembled the youth council, responsible for fielding the concerns of young
people as the high school neared opening day. The youth council would
meet biweekly, while being facilitated by a youth advocate from the TAC.
The idea was that when the school was up and running, the youth council members (that were in sixth, seventh, and eighth grades at the time)
would transition to the youth councils of each of the high schools in the
multiplex. Organizers from the Crib Collective and LVCDC secured the
position of young people in the remaining months of the initiative. Both
youth advocates from the Crib Collective were college students, responsible
for facilitating youth meetings and providing report-backs to the TAC. The
concept behind this was when the TAC shifted its leadership responsibility
to the four schools, the task of the youth advocate and the youth committee was to ensure permanent student input and participation in governance
throughout the life of the high school. By way of Cynthia's RFP, the TAC
required the four high schools to demonstrate how young people will be
included in the daily decision-making of each school.

Students, with little knowledge of each other's culture are often skeptical of engaging each other inside classroom space and school grounds.
Because residents in both neighborhoods know little about the other's community and culture, a concerted effort by the TAC and community members
was needed to secure school support. In fact, when the idea that African-
American and Mexican-Americans would be going to the same school, some
members of the youth council felt the concept would never work. However,
with the involvement of the youth advocate, many members of the community realized the importance of interracial, cross-cultural collaboration
to make the project work.

For the first couple of youth council meetings, it was difficult to get young people from Little Village and North Lawndale to engage a conversation. First, the initial tensions of language and unfamiliarity became clear as young people from both groups sat on separate sides of the room as the youth advocates explained the purpose of the council. In order to get the youth on the same page in understanding why having a peaceful and constructive coexistence process was critical to the development of the process, the youth advocates had to communicate the history of the two communities. From this discussion, young people began to understand the ability of their neighborhoods to work collaboratively. The young people were also deeply affected by the situation with the attendance boundaries

> The most difficult time on the TAC was during the issues of the attendance boundaries. LVCDC and LCDC are political organizations: they want to be seen as good by their constituents. (Both were) reluctant to ruffle the feathers of the community in that way. Even when people were being outright racist . . . I would've like to have seen the involvement of a lot more of the smaller grassroots community organizations from both communities. Although CDCs have a lot of resources, and access to resources, because they are political organizations and political in nature they may not be able to push the boundaries . . . The way that a small grassroots organization can. (Aquil Charlton interview, July 23, 2012)

Unfortunately, despite the intentions of the TAC, the youth council never came to fruition beyond its initial meetings. Community development corporations (CDCs), while having access to resources, played a pivotal role throughout the process, but were also imbued in the politics of race, place, and school. Reflecting on what outweighed an authentic, community-driven process that would include North Lawndale, he felt that CPS's rushed timeline prevented the groups from engaging in processes that would benefit both communities.

The Story of the Five Worlds

As members of the TAC and design teams, we were required to attend a series of workshops with members from the other three design teams. One of the meetings was opened with a conversation with the primary architect of the school. He explained that as part of remaining accountable to the core values of the hunger strike, community members (along with the original members of the hunger strike) were given disposable cameras to look at various schools across the city to investigate school buildings. The idea was to create a space that was reflective of both communities and permanent reminders of the struggle to build a school. From the lengthy conversations and meetings with the group of architects, the number of designs was narrowed to four. The final design was an architectural interpretation of the numerological representations of the hunger strike and the Aztec story of the five worlds.

The Aztec legend speaks of the elements of fire, air, water, and earth. Each element in the school building is represented by a color that adorns the bricks in each of the schools. The bricks in the multicultural arts school are green, representing the earth. The bricks in SOJO are red, representing the world of fire (also referenced as the color of change). Bricks in the math, science, and technology building are blue, representing water. The world language school has purple colored bricks, representative of the air. Stained glass with a block of each color are throughout the school library and are beneath the school sign at the main entrance. The fifth world is represented in a sixty-foot sundial structure in the middle of the building. To commemorate the hunger strike, points are marked in the interior of the cone. From May 13 to June 1 (the original nineteen days of the strike) the sun (by way of a skylight) hits a dot marked on the interior of the cone on each of the nineteen days. On June 1, the dot reaches the center of the cone and is reflected as a beam of light on a compass on the floor of the dial (www.midwestconstruction.com/features/archive/0501_feature1.asp). The sundial is used as a collective meeting space for all four schools. Schools may use the space for project displays, art projects, student meetings, and community forum.

Commemorating the nineteen days of the hunger strike, the entire school rests on a nineteen-degree angle. Fourteen trees have been placed at the south end of the school to represent the fourteen hunger strikers who went the duration of the nineteen days. A patch of tall grass rests on the north end of the campus, acknowledging the original site of Camp Cesar Chavez (site of the hunger strike). The entrance of the school has a mosaic recognizing the communities of North Lawndale and Little Village, to remind students of the struggles of both communities in making the high school a reality. Murals created by students adorn the hallways in each of the schools, calling for community unity and recognition of the struggle to create the high school. The art wing of the building is dedicated to world-renowned African-American sculptor and printmaker Elizabeth Catlett (who also attended the dedication before her passing in 2012). All of these design structures, while symbolic, are important to the historical record. While the building is not an institution of learning without the students, teachers, and community members, design structures such as these are important in that they provide a constant visual connection to the struggle to create the high school.

In terms of the day-to-day administration of the school, a process intended to ground each school in unity was the idea of the fifth world, where administration would conduct meetings and coplan activities and curriculum for all of the four schools. Some elements of the fifth world are evident, as sports teams are shared across campuses, and the principals still meet weekly to address logistical and budgetary concerns. However, the original fifth world was envisioned as a space to reflect the values of the hunger strike and the possibilities as the years advanced in the school. Rito and Jaime were most disappointed by the process never coming to fruition.

> The way that we translated those surveys, into four themed independent schools and we did not tie them together in a way that was comprehensive. In a way that was based on any type of values. In a way that actually reflected the architecture of the fifth world. And that fifth world community committee never got established to sort of hold the four schools accountable to creative vision and purpose. And we lost that battle . . . and every school, every principal and every staff became focused on its on survival . . . In hindsight Social Justice, the values of the hunger strike, the language of the community which mentioned the issues of equity of access, and understanding issues of power should have been the theme for all four schools. It should have been that fifth world theme that harnessed and tethered all four schools. Instead of, what happened was each school did its own thing its own fulfillment of its own vision and one school was left to do the values of the hunger strike. And I'm not sure if we interpreted those surveys correctly. I'm not sure if we interpreted what the community envisioned correctly. Quite frankly we didn't vet the translation of the surveys to ask the community is this what you want? (Martinez interview, July 9, 2012)

As the fifth world never came to fruition beyond the narrative architecture and the mundane functions of any school, the idea was rooted in having physical and procedural testament to the values of the hunger strike. However, it is also reflective of the myriad ideas that never came to fruition. As this happens with many new schools, it is disappointing to know that this particular vision could not be realized.

A Question of Governance

Dating back to the Chicago school reforms of 1988, Local School Councils (LSCs) have been an embattled entity in CPS. Originally begun as a way to ensure community control and accountability by providing a council consisting of parents, community members, teachers, students, and the principal, LSCs were able to approve four-year principal contracts and provide final approval of the budget. Originally LSCs were trained by community organizations to ensure accountability from the central office. Once funding expired to compensate community organizations for the trainings, CPS resumed responsibilities for the trainings. While some of the facilitators were very adept at their occupations, many were unable to convey the necessary importance and utility of LSCs. While some remain active and central to galvanizing resistance against current neoliberal policies in CPS, others took a beating in the press for their mismanagement of funds, cronyism, and serving at the behest of the principal. At the time, the mayor's office (under the second Daley) engaged in a frontal attack on LSCs in 1995 with the advent of mayoral control. Providing the mayor's office the final say on school issues, the power of LSCs was curtailed to some extent. Under the 1995 reforms, if the mayor needed something to happen at a particular school for the purposes of patronage, nepotism, or voter support, there was a clearer path by which to enact his will.

In relation to the TAC and design teams, there was an initial discussion among both groups as whether or not to have LSCs on the campus. Because the Hispanic Democratic Organization (HDO, at the time an ally organization to the Daley administration) was making attempts to encroach on the twenty-second ward, some members of the design teams felt that it was best not to have LSCs, further limiting HDOs reach and preventing the advent of unilateral political support by way of LSC elections. Because the mayor wanted to further limit the scope of LSCs, small schools were not allowed to have Advisory Local School Councils (ALSCs) that only had recommendation powers on issues of principal hiring and budget. Where this did not pose a problem in the first years of the school, it almost proved deadly in later years. Discussed in detail in chapter 7, the victories and losses throughout the process of building a school are both immediate and cyclical.

Chapter 3

Counterstory as Praxis

Confronting Success and Failure on the Design Team

The combination of counterstory and the tenets of critical race praxis allow for a space to theorize on the real and perceived tensions between groups (researchers, community members, community organizers, CPS, CPS partners, etc.) along the lines of race, class, ethnicity, power, and educational policy. As the design team got closer to the final deposit of the proposal to CPS, SOJO and the three other schools were pulled into the revolving door of neoliberal housing and educational by way of Renaissance 2010. Connecting business interests to educational development, the policy has created a veneer that continues to marginalize and isolate low-income/working-class African-American and Latino/a communities. Paired with the responsibilities of preparing the final RFP, the layers of the process included a host of participants entering and exiting the process. From my own participation on the design team, I slowly learned that solidarity was a contested phenomenon, challenging me to understand collective over singular desires to speak truth to power. As members of TAC actively grappled with the potential tensions between both communities, the work of the design teams intensified as CPS began to present a rushed timeline as the summer of 2005 (opening day) approached.

Preparing a Proposal

Cynthia's approach to developing a Greater Lawndale–specific (La Villita and North Lawndale) RFP was critical in maintaining the values generated in the strike. Though at first it might seem mundane to pepper the values of the hunger strike throughout the language of the document, it became critical in resisting CPS bureaucracy. As CHSRI created a template, the CHSRI administrators allowed Cynthia Nambo to create a RFP that specifically addressed the needs of the Greater Lawndale community.

> The Chicago Public Schools, the CHSRI Advisory Board and the Little Village Transition Advisory Council are seeking applicants who desire to plan and implement a new small high in the Little Village and North Lawndale Communities.
>
> Proposals may be submitted by design teams who intend to meet the desired goals of the Chicago High School Redesign Initiative (CHSRI). Design teams should include representatives from a variety of stakeholders, including teachers who plan to teach in the school, and optimally a principal candidate. The school design teams should address the Initiative's seven (7) autonomies and other design criteria, including a governance model that supports both autonomy and accountability. (Nambo 2004, 8)

Headings in the RFP included a "principles and values" section that lists the fourteen values of the strike listed in chapter 1. The four principles of "community ownership, cross cultural/multicultural, global community, and learning" were listed along with the values in the beginning of the document. Providing an example of the explicit attempt to engage both communities the cross cultural/multiracial states, "African-American, Latino and students of varied cultures will be welcomed equally; so too, all will be encouraged to develop a sense of ownership of the school" (4). Where CHSRI had a section dedicated to its "seven autonomies" (budget, staffing, curriculum, leadership, schedule, facilities, and co-curricular activities) Cynthia created a new section titled "Other Design Criteria" that would allow for design teams to demonstrate how the fourteen values of the hunger strike would be implemented in the day-to-day operations of the schools.

Convincing CHSRI that their seven autonomies were too general and commonplace, Cynthia's additions and reconfigurations allowed for space to engage the values of the larger community-driven effort to secure the school. On, the surface, some of the language looked commonplace in RFPs for schools, while other sections were explicit about the specific issues in North Lawndale and La Villita. Her inclusion of language that specifically named both communities and racial/ethnic groups allowed for particular innovations to be included in SOJO's proposal. This particular layer of bureaucracy provided us with some cover by way of the Chicago-based

CHSRI administrators. Because this particular group was sympathetic to the values of the hunger strike, they demonstrated a willingness to keep community at the center of the effort. Coupled with the fact that they were the primary funding partner, their influence allowed Cynthia and later our design team the opportunity to explicitly describe the process and implementation plans specific to the needs of students from both communities. For our particular proposal, these sections allowed us to defend the process of "accountability agreements," a "building sharing agreement" the concerted efforts of community members by way of the original committees, the advisory committee and the TAC allowed the necessary space for Cynthia to develop her own components. In order for the proposals to be approved by the TAC, each design, based on the language of the RFP, was required to thread the principles and values of the hunger strike throughout their proposal. To some, the upholding of the values was thought to be reserved solely for SOJO. However, Cynthia's authorship made it so that any perspective design team needed to ensure that community concerns were threaded throughout their proposal.

At the same time there are particularities that deserve explicit attention in the creation of a school. Due to the technical language of the proposal, CPS felt as if it could assert itself in the process. At almost every juncture, CPS would "remind" the TAC and the design teams that this was a CPS-"sanctioned" process and all of the final requirements still had to be in concert with its rules and regulations. Despite CPS's attempts to regulate the process, we were unusually positioned to challenge its advancements through the language of the RFP. Paired with the TAC's stated commitment to the values and principles of the strike, it wasn't an easy task for CPS to insert its will. However, the one place where CPS could insert its resolve was in the enforcement of timelines.

Granted, this was not always a smooth process. Tempers flare and personalities clash when stakes are as high as they were in this development. Where most of the members of the TAC were on the same page regarding the community initiative, there were arguments on how much credence should be given to CPS's whims and requests. While she was active in the process, Cynthia was able to quell much of the tension by way of the protocols implemented to vet the proposals from the design teams. Because I was outside of the TAC process, it would often appear as if CPS would take advantage of these tensions by marking some of the TAC members as unruly or "difficult to talk to." This could easily descend into chaos if not for members reminding each other of the uniqueness and critical nature of the current moment. Nevertheless, members of the TAC would continually find themselves at crossroads when it came between choosing accountability to the community initiative and compliance with CPS policy. It became especially difficult when the people responsible for communicating CPS policy and mandates to the design team in many cases were African-American and Latino/a. Even more troubling was the fact that many understood how hegemonic bureaucracies derail community initiatives. On numerous occasions we were "advised" on how not to "ruffle the feathers" of CPS in creating the high school. In the neoliberal sense, they felt that they were "doing us a favor." In reality, it often felt like CPS was keeping up its end of the bargain as derailing agents of the state, intent on never having the school come to fruition as the community intended.

To Create a Design Team

As another layer to the process, once the Advisory Board transitioned into the TAC, there were meetings held at all the feeder schools based on the attendance boundaries. During this time I attended numerous meetings at surrounding feeder schools (Corkery, Eli Whitney, Hughes, and Mason). Understanding that there would have to be a concerted effort to recruit members from North Lawndale, Rito went into high gear in the attempt to recruit students and parents. From this moment in time we were able to add Eric "Rico" Gutstein to the group. One of his earliest recollections in coming to the process was a conversation with me about how to bring the school to fruition after the hunger strike. In addition to his position as a university professor, he was teaching a math course at a local K–8 school close to Camp Chavez. From our conversation he contacted Cynthia and Jaime and requested that they interview him, because he was interested in working on the design team. The three of them met at a restaurant in La Villita and discussed what he had been doing with his K–8 classroom and why he was interested in working on the design teams. Upon hearing his story, they invited him to join the process (Eric Gutstein interview, July 30, 2012).

Because the design teams required membership from teachers who would potentially work at the school, I volunteered to recruit teachers I knew throughout the city. I contacted two teachers I know who were doing impactful work in their various locales. To my delight, they were both interested. The two teachers we were most interested in were newer teachers (one taught for three years and the other was in his first year of teaching). Unfortunately for us, one of the teachers only had a certification that would let her teach up to ninth grade while the other teacher decided to remain at his current institution. Although a devastating blow to our initial process, we continued with our work as the design team.

At the neighborhood level, the community forums were the engine by which to recruit parents to the design team. After a few meetings at Eli Whitney and Corkery, in addition to Rito Martinez (our principal candidate), Rico Gutstein, and me, we were able to recruit three parents (Alicia Serrano, Marisol Damaso, and Pat Christopher), a veteran teacher (Steve Yannias), one concerned community member (Lizandra Linares), a consultant (Carol Lieber, secured by Cynthia Nambo by way of CHSRI funds), and one assistant principal (Berta Arredondo) to the design team. Despite some expressed interest, we were not able to recruit parents from North Lawndale. This became problematic throughout our process, because without their input we did not have the authentic community engagement needed to represent both communities.

At the height of our design-team membership, CPS required attendance at numerous meetings and institutes. Additionally the TAC (by way of Cynthia Nambo) created a series of workshops called the Praxis Institute, designed to walk design teams through the process of creating the proposals. Due to family and work obligations (design team participation was on a volunteer basis), there were many instances where design team members were unable to make it to meetings. Because these meetings were so frequent (anywhere from one to three times per week), it became difficult to stay abreast of the newest developments and requirements. Coupled with the fact that some of the CPS-required meetings did not provide interpreter services, they could be daunting for community members whose primary language is Spanish. Taking all of this into consideration, our numbers began to dwindle. As we closely approached the deadline submission date for the proposal, the remaining design team members were Rito, Rico, and myself. In hindsight, some of the messiness of authentic including community members has to take into consideration the real-world obligations families and community members may have. Throughout our time on the design team this became increasingly difficult as the process moved forward. In similar fashion, it is incorrect to assume that community members are less committed because of their inability to attend meetings. In all truth, the fact that I had a full course-load buyout was one of the primary reasons I was able to attend a large percentage of the meetings. In another situation I could be in a similar predicament to many of the other members of the design team. Paired with the pressure of the ensuing deadline, our work as the design team could at times feel rushed and haphazard.

The Weak Kitty in the Litter

Returning to the political gamesmanship that is often included in contested agreements between community stakeholders and large school districts, we were always provided with some type of colorful commentary from the central office. Usually passed off as snide comments by disconnected central office bureaucrats, they were taken with a grain of salt. As annoying as they could be at the moment, I began to think of it as the subtle psychological game intended to produce doubt in the minds of members of the design team.

One occasion remained on our minds as members of the design teams throughout the process. After a meeting with the advisory board/TAC, a representative for ONS asked us, "What are you going to do about the weak kitty in the litter?" From our puzzled looks she continued to state that one of these proposals was not going to make the cut as the TAC approved the proposals. For those of us on the SOJO design team, we took it as a direct shot to our process, referring to earlier comments about the utility of social justice and questioning its merits as a theme for a high school. Similar to the neoliberal stance on competition, her comment indicated that the winners and losers were predetermined. If this was the case, it begged the questions: Was CPS giving lip service to the community because central office had final say on the process? Was this process mere window dressing to get charter schools in the building under Renaissance 2010? Would CPS claim that our proposals were rejected because we were not in some newly concocted compliance? In an intense political process such as this, it is not uncommon for groups to fall victim to their own paranoia. Though we could only assume her intent in the conversation, the subtle undertones deserved attention in this situation; we understood that at no point could we let our guard down to the central office. Agreeing that we would move forward as the design team, we kept this in mind as the deadline for the proposal submission drew near.

Putting Research to Work: My SOJO Fact-Finding Mission

Trying our best to shake off the "weak kitty" commentary, we transformed it into a rallying cry for the design team. Knowing we had to get back to work, I took some cues from the advisory committee and the TAC. When they went across the country to visit schools that were created by way of community efforts, I embarked on a fact-finding mission to schools that were part of the small schools movement. As members of the TAC traveled to cities across the country that operationalized the small schools concept, our idea on the design team was to do the same. Utilizing a perk from my position as university faculty, I was awarded an internal fellowship. Making the attempt to remain accountable to the community-driven initiative via the design team, my application to the fellowship specifically was centered in engaged community-based research, noting the series of events emanating from the hunger strike as an authentic example of community resistance to neoliberal forces. Luckily, for the purpose of my work, the entity providing the fellowship encouraged projects that reimagined traditional school/university relationships. Personally, the fellowship represented the opportunity to provide an example of accountability in a community/university partnership. Instead of a monetary award in terms of direct liquid assets, the fellowship provided a series of course buyouts for the entire year. Being released from my teaching duties for the year opened my schedule to work specifically with the design team.

Additionally, because SOJO had a particular focus on social justice, it became important to go to other schools across the country to learn about their efforts to create environments for justice-centered education. Some schools I traveled to I knew through a network of educational justice organizations and colleagues (Banana Kelly High School in the Bronx; El Puente Academy for Peace and Justice in Williamsburg, Brooklyn; Bushwick School for Social Justice; Communication Arts and Sciences Academy at Berkeley High School), while others I came in contact with via personal relationships cultivated over the years (East Oakland Community High School; Tucson Social Justice Education Project; and Raza Studies Program also in Tucson).

During this time there were shared themes across all the schools I visited. The first was the fact that every school operated as a public institution. Second was the fact that veteran instructors and principals were committed to instructional support of new teachers. Team-taught courses were encouraged in addition to developing mentoring systems for new teachers. Third was a commitment to create a caring environment for students above local, state, and federal requirements. Last, all of the schools and programs had an explicit goal to develop critical consciousness in students and families. Above all, because of their commitment to a radical reimagining of education, they were all contested by systems of the state. Almost in a strange form of foreshadowing for the duration of SOJO's existence, every program I visited had at one point been threatened with closure. In the most extreme instances, some of the schools and programs were shuttered due to their perceived radical stance on education or low performance on state assessment exams (Raza Studies in Tucson and East Oakland Community High School).

All of the programs were generous enough to share their proposals, curriculum, and instructional strategies. These were extremely useful as we began to develop each section of the proposal. Of particular use to the design team was the ability to observe these schools in their various locales. El Puente was the oldest school I visited, with its origins in the mid-1990s, while East Oakland Community High School (EOC) started the year before SOJO opened its doors (2004). Teachers, administrators, and students were curious and excited to hear about what was happening in Chicago and were excited about our progress.

Final Touches

A running joke we would often use about the multiplex and SOJO was that every inch of the building reflected the revolutionary commitment to develop justice-centered education in La Villita and North Lawndale; I would often joke that instead of the Greater Lawndale High School for Social Justice, the school should be named the Che Lumumba Institute for Revolutionary Practice in Education. Whereas this brought laughs in some of the early advisory board/TAC meetings, some members actually liked where I was going with the idea. I remember at one meeting there were a couple of us who were talking about having the school mascot be the Macheteros. We continued our pipe dream with a giant floor painting on the basketball court with two arms crossed, holding machetes with blood dripping from them and running down the arms. I can remember yelling, "Now that's a *real* school right there!" Among the laughter a person from another design team talked about having a painted trail on the floor of the school and calling it the Ho Chi Minh Trail. Coupled with the architecture narrative of the school, we thought about how novel it would be for us. Soon after revealing our pipe dreams to the group, someone gave us a serious look and said, "You do remember that this *is* CPS right?" From there we stopped for a second and snapped back into the reality that they were right, despite our illusions.

For our specific proposal, the language of the RFP allowed for a couple of innovations to SOJO's daily operation. One came by way of a curricular innovation known as a colloquium. Through one of Rito's visits to a selective enrollment school in the city, he observed a structured-day innovation that provided students with a self-selected course that explored an issue relevant to their lives. The colloquium structure provides an opportunity to enhance student knowledge of subject matter in a nontraditional setting.

Students would not receive grades or course credit for the colloquium. Instead, they would have the opportunity to earn service-learning hours—forty of which are required for graduation from a CPS high school. Also, the meeting schedule for the colloquium is significantly different from that of traditional classes. Classes would be offered once a week on weeks where there were no holidays or system-mandated institute days (e.g., report card pickup, staff development, etc.). The idea was that if students could self-select a topic of interest and generate topics for subsequent colloquia it would enhance school culture by becoming a place where students could associate with genuine interest and engagement.

In addition to the colloquium offering, as a college preparatory high school, Rico and I promised to teach at the school as an effective way to grant early college credit to high school students. Similar to college bridge programs that provide similar offerings, our idea was to dually enroll SOJO students in our respective university, providing them with transferrable general education courses they could use toward graduation at the college they chose to attend. My original offering at SOJO would be a sociology course, while Rico would teach a math course.

Instead of traditional lesson planning with goals, objectives, enduring understandings, and state-standards alignment, Rico came up with the idea of what we would come to call the 3Cs (classical, community, and critical knowledge). He originally thought of this as the integrated math program curriculum (IMP) we decided to use wasn't critical, but allowed the space to make adjustments to engage math from a Freirean perspective. Situated in critical mathematics, the 3Cs were a process that would allow teachers in all content areas to use an alternative lesson-planning strategy that takes into account the value of developing in-depth knowledge of self and community.

> When I've written about that, I've always stated that they are not new ideas. They have just been underelaborated and under-theorized with respect to math education. I make no claim (to them) . . . to me that came from an analysis of what happened in critical mathematics which I use synonymously with teaching math for social justice, which I use synonymously with reading and writing the world with mathematics. I know that there's so many different ways people understand these things, that there isn't one set definition for whatever, so I just use these three terms synonymously and have my own definitions of what I

mean. In studying Freire I understood that actually Freire's work kind of synthesized these three C's together: community, critical, and classical knowledge in a way that started with community knowledge . . . but that supported to strongly develop critical knowledge . . . it brought the three together . . . If you're gonna learn math, you're gonna study context, why don't you study about the context of your lives. This is what Freire has done . . . my understanding of these 3 Cs really comes from that . . . reflecting on the practice in math ed and the theoretical and practical limitations with respect to a Freirean model which really synthesizes these three . . . that's where it came from. (Eric Gutstein interview, July 30, 2012)

In addition to IMP, we also had Patty Buenrostro (one of the *huelgistas*) on board who taught the curriculum for years at a local public school in the city. Coupled with the 3Cs, the idea was to demonstrate the home communities of our students as places of value instead of places of deficit (community knowledge), sites where issues can be collectively examined and addressed (critical knowledge), while meeting any benign standard or assessment set forward by local, state, or federal government. If not for the spaces created by Cynthia's intentional inclusion of community concerns, these innovations would have been more difficult to justify.

Speaking "With" or Speaking "For?"

One of the most contentious moments in the entire design team/TAC process was the wrongful inclusion of the high school under the policy of Renaissance 2010. As the community-driven initiative predates Renaissance 2010 by three years, the policy's intent stands in direct opposition to the values developed during the hunger strike guiding the group into the design team/TAC process. Mentioned briefly in the introduction and chapter 1, our working knowledge of Renaissance 2010 brought discomfort among members of the TAC and the SOJO design team. As a policy rooted in neoliberal urbanism and corporate educational reform, the policy stood as an outright attempt to further marginalize low-income/working-class Black and Brown communities through a convergence of housing and educational policy.

Operating from the report "Left Behind" created by the Civic Committee of the Commercial Club of Chicago (the conglomerate representing multinational corporate business interests in the city), CPS proposed to target up to seventy "chronically underperforming" schools for "transformation" into one hundred schools with the distinction of either charter, contract or performance school by 2010. The mandate was introduced to the press in July of 2004, at a meeting at the Commercial Club, dubbing the policy Renaissance 2010. Where charters are granted by the state, contract schools have a different distinction in that they are a designation for individuals or groups that have secured individual contracts with the city to create schools. Because the vast majority of charter schools are not unionized, proliferation of charters had the potential to engage in union-busting as fewer teachers would have access to membership in the Chicago Teachers Union (CTU). Contract schools are a close cousin to charters with regard to funding formulas, the distinct difference lies in the direct partnership with the city, as charters are traditionally granted by the state. Despite their classification as public schools, both charters and contracts are not required to provide union protection. Currently, the largest contract institution in Chicago is the Academy of Urban School Leadership (AUSL). Schools in the performance category were another manifestation of schools, aimed at giving principals and teachers some levels of autonomy regarding curriculum and schedule. Simultaneously, the internal understanding was to lessen the city's financial commitment to education through the use of partners that could in turn use their contributions to education as tax subsidies (through the federal tax code's provision for charitable donations). Returning to the public sphere, said manifestations were posited to community residents as Chicago Public School moving to provide "choice" and "options" in the "education marketplace" (www.cps.edu/NewSchools/Pages/ONS.aspx).

The first sight of this experiment would take place in a collective of rapidly gentrifying African-American neighborhoods known as the mid-South region. Consisting of the geographic neighborhoods of Kenwood, Oakland, Grand Boulevard, and Douglass, twenty of the twenty-two schools in the four-neighborhood area were targeted for closure or restructuring in the aforementioned forms. Fortunately, due to the collective efforts of community organizations and a team of collaborating researchers, the first effort of the experiment was curtailed. Thanks to their efforts it was discovered that many of the schools targeted for reconfiguration were performing at or exceeding the standards set forward by the state. One specific community organization, the Kenwood Oakland Community Organization (KOCO) staged a sleep-in at CPS's central office building. Coupled with the work of Pauline Lipman, their efforts garnered attention resulting in the curtailing of the original rollout plan targeting twenty schools. Instead CPS targeted ten schools, reconfiguring the vast majority to charters and contract schools.

Critical to this process is the intimate relationship to the housing market. Sited extensively in Arrastia (2007), Lipman (2003, 2011, 2012), and Smith (2006, 2008, 2012), because housing stock is key in attracting business interests in the city, schooling becomes an important conduit in solidifying long-term investment in schools. Because the main determinant of a family's home purchase are the schools in the perspective neighborhood, the mid-South region became a hotbed for gentrification, most notably through the mass destruction of public housing through the Chicago Housing Authority's (CHA) Plan for Transformation (Lipman 2011). The mixed-income strategy employed to redevelop public housing in Chicago is a product of this thinking. Touted as a $1.6 billion plan, its aim is to redevelop areas once occupied by high-rise public housing as mixed-income communities. As housing stock in the redeveloped areas will be distributed in thirds among very low-income, moderate-income, and market-rate homes, questions arise as dubious qualifications have been placed on the low-income group (*Chicago Tribune*, September 22, 2004). To receive any of the homes in the recent developments, public housing families have to go through a battery of screenings for health (specifically for substance abuse), employment (applicants must now work at least thirty hours per week unless they are unable to or are in a training/educational program), and criminal activity (a person cannot rent an apartment if anyone in the household has a felony conviction). In the "Plan for Transformation" schools are framed as an important part of the plan, and the change in housing has been projected to mean an increase in families of moderate and affluent incomes. Because this requires strategic planning on the part of CPS, the converging of Renaissance 2010 and the Plan for Transformation was critical in bringing the larger neoliberal plan into fruition. Despite the provisions for low-income families in the new mixed-income communities, the aforementioned health, employment, and criminal compliances help to carefully sanitize the community marketed to newcomers. Schools, as the final frontier, provide the necessary push for buyers to take the final step in securing life in the city. Fortunately for the families that remain in some of the targeted areas, a collective of community organizations have been able to develop strategies to contest the efforts of CPS.

While not part of the policy, CPS wrongly included the Little Village/Lawndale Campus in its Renaissance 2010 literature. Recognizing our opposition to the policy, it was admitted to us by an ONS official that any new school was considered a Renaissance 2010 school, as it was the new blanket policy that ushered any new school to CPS. Yet again, the revolving door of central office policy shifted its rhetoric, subsuming existing community efforts to create quality schools for historically disinvested communities. By including the Little Village/Lawndale Campus in their policy rhetoric, it automatically affiliated the efforts to create the multiplex with a policy designed to further limit the educational opportunities for residents in poor Black and Brown communities.

Upon noticing CPS claim of the Little Village/Lawndale in Renaissance 2010, Rico Gutstein (university professor and member of the SOJO design team) quickly asked to speak to the TAC regarding CPS wrongful inclusion. Upon explaining the problematic undercurrent of Renaissance 2010, the TAC requested a community hearing on the policy. Held at Eli Whitney School (one of the feeder schools for the complex), community members, coupled with communities affected by Renaissance 2010, provided public testimony against the policy. Upon hearing the results of the community hearing, the TAC requested a meeting with CEO Arne Duncan, ONS, and the CPS demographer.

The demographer opened the session with a discussion of the boundaries and the new configurations to achieve the seventy/thirty limits set forth by the district (original compliance with the consent decree was interpreted by CPS that the school could be no more than 70% Latino/a and 30% African-American). Soon after the demographer's presentation, the CEO arrived late with another representative from his office. Following the demographer, a letter was read by members of the TAC discussing the problematic nature of Renaissance 2010 and its relationship to corporate neoliberal education reform by way of gentrification, union-busting, and disinvestment. At the time I sat directly behind the CEO when he delivered his response to the TAC's concerns.

As expected, his response was uninformed and painfully despondent. He claimed that there were "union shops" in the newly proposed charter schools. He also suggested that Du Sable High School was not in a gentrifying neighborhood, despite being across the street from a site that at one time was the largest public housing unit in the world (the Robert Taylor Homes). The commentary continued to state how some schools were closed or transitioned due to underperformance and underenrollment. Despite his intimate knowledge of KOCO's opposition to the policy, one of his officials stated that KOCO's response was hastily constructed and wrongheaded. The end of meeting was inconclusive, but the potential principals from each of the design teams were promised another meeting with officials from Duncan's office (ibid.)

The entire time while I sat behind him, I was reeling with anger and wanted to lash out. The inaccuracies of his answers were disgusting and paternalistic. At the same time, I wanted to respect the TAC's process and not further jeopardize their relationship with the central office. Speaking "for" the group at this point had the potential to derail the process, as CPS prides itself on being able to enforce absolute power when able. Ideologically the hunger strike represented a mere ripple in its hegemonic power. Since it did not consult with the TAC before Duncan's arrival, I didn't have the necessary clearance to engage Duncan in a way that directly challenged his answers. Additionally, because I was not a TAC member, I knew any wrong move could intensify the current tension-filled relationship with CPS. Cloaked behind a public veneer of politeness, the clashes between community process and CPS deadlines were coming to a head as opening day approached. A random response from a design team member had the potential to further derail the process set forth by the TAC. Where this was a prime opportunity to speak truth to power, it was also under the guise of respecting community process without engaging in a frontal attack on central office brass. To this day, the fact that I did not offer a response still haunts me.

Tiffany Childress's reflections are essential to my memory of this moment, due to a conversation we had following the meeting with Duncan. When I commented on the issues with Renaissance 2010, she asked me directly why I didn't have those responses when Duncan was in our presence. My only response at the moment was that I didn't have permission from the group and did not want to derail the process already set forth by the TAC. Her recollection of the moment echoed some of my sentiment.

> As a young organizer, it was exciting and overwhelming at the same time because I could see the complexity and how political one has to be and knowing who's in the room and when you should speak and when you shouldn't speak. . . . (Tiffany Childress interview July 31, 2012)

Contrasting our position, Rito Martinez's approach was more diplomatic. At the time he was fresh off similar experiences as a principal intern in a principal training program. His view was in concert with some members of the TAC, noting how problematic Renaissance 2010 was for the rest of the city, while also understanding the spaces that could be navigated during the process. At the school level, because the policy divided the new schools into charter, contract, or performance schools, CPS financial equation for SOJO presented a number of direct issues that would affect staffing. As a new school, a healthy combination of veteran and new teachers is critical in providing instructional support for new teachers. If it is a new school with majority new teachers, the risk for staff turnover is high due to lack of support and burnout. Understanding this immediately, Rito felt the key was to have

> The intentionality and flexibility to have progressive veteran teachers that could really stay on and support younger teachers and really create a school is critical. To me the battle was more about that than Renaissance 2010. (Martinez interview, July 9, 2012)

In relation to budget this was a critical element, because CPS gave us the option of using a lump-sum equation where the school would have autonomy in curriculum but wouldn't be able to pay veteran teachers due to the lump sum given to each school. Under the core positions equation, teacher salaries are based on enrollment instead of a lump-sum amount. To ensure that school culture would be strong, one of our small victories in this moment was the ability to be funded by the core positions equation. Despite our disagreement with CPS at the macro level, the flexibility to retain the teachers we wanted was critical. In school development, there are few things worse than having interest from a teacher that you can't keep due to budget constraints.

Nevertheless, my frustrations were evident, understanding that our individual victory as SOJO would not impact the continued displacement and marginalization of other low-income/working-class communities across the city. In a meager attempt to express my frustrations about the event, I went to my office and offered the following field notes on my experience.

∾

The reality of school design is a trip—the politics are nasty as they are amazing. In my case you get a situation of regular folks trying to do right by their communities in getting a school off the ground that addresses their need to provide a quality education for young people. Over the last three and a half years, things have spiraled in a whirlwind of mess around the attempt to ensure the principles of a grassroots initiative to create a community high school. The initiative started with a group of parents, grandparents, and concerned community members who set out on a hunger strike, protesting the failure of CPS to grant the community a high school after being promised a school in 1998. While other high-end, selective enrollment high schools were developed in other areas across the city, they were overlooked. Needless to say, when the community

got serious with central office through a hunger strike, they decided to build the
high school. Now we're knee deep in shit trying to remain true to the initiative.
Since it's a public school, CPS has their hands all in our shit with nonsensical
compliances, requirements, and a new arcane policy that's designed to attract
White folks back to the city through the promise of good schools and new homes.
It's become so ridiculous it's like we can't even take a shit without these chumps
trying to push something on us. Nevertheless, the community has moved forward
in holding CPS accountable to the initiative. However, shit is still not sweet.
We almost fucked ourselves by getting tricked into signing off on the city's new
housing-schools initiative (Renaissance 2010).

It's the political chumps who just seem to fuck it up mercilessly with bullshit
politics and the realities of seedy bureaucracies that prevent folks from doing what
they have to do. And the veneer the central office chumps operate under is so slick.
So shiny. All the bells and whistles with no substance. In the end, community folks
get played because they get overwhelmed with the shininess and slick language
diversions by central office folks who narrowly escape with their asses because they
control the language of power for the entire time. It's a heavy lesson in organiza-
tion for grassroots communities of color who decide to go into this school thing.
For all who do, BEWARE OF CENTRAL OFFICE! Organize yourselves on a
united front when dealing with these snakes. Treat them like murderous bastards
who have a .45 caliber at the table and will blow your brains out as soon as you
turn your back. There are no friends here. No room for "nice talk." Shit is too
serious. Treat this with the utmost seriousness. Lives are in the balance. Continue
to strategize and organize on whatever issues are at hand. Do not become fooled
by double-talk. These fuckers are playing for keeps and so should you.

≈

However incoherent my reflections may seem, at the time they were my attempt to make sense of the meeting and the ideologies operating under the politically correct veneer of politeness. Using colorful language like "chumps" and "snakes" were indicative of my feelings at the moment. To this day I am unsure if I made the right decision by not speaking out. Coupled with my personal understandings of city politics, the instance with Duncan in the LVCDC office is the example of how power can deflect, regroup, and move subversively. For these reasons, CPS in every instance should be greeted with a healthy amount of skepticism. In many instances I tried to forget the experience, but the realities of the moment were a constant reminder of how counterstory and race praxis challenges us to engage the practice of healing from wounds inflicted during tumultuous moments in struggle.

Chapter 4

Paper Proposals Do Not Equal Real Life

Race Praxis and High School Creation

The nuts and bolts of building a staff and school culture is a challenging task when pressed against a short timeline. From our positions as members of the design team the new challenge was to put place, time, names, and faces to the proposal submitted to the TAC. Once we were granted final approval from the TAC, it was now our job to make concrete the practice of bringing SOJO to fruition. The CRP tenets of the performative and the material are critical in this juncture as time was more the challenge than issues set forward from CPS. More than abstract theorizing, the "nuts and bolts" of preparing a school for opening day creates an intimate relationship between the meticulous and mundane.

Final TAC Approval

The TAC required the final design team presentations to be public. In compliance with the Illinois Open Meetings Act, each design team presented to the TAC in a public forum that was held at the LVCDC office. Because the majority of contact between design teams took place at the Praxis Institutes, we were unaware of the particular progress of each individual team. While there was never an air of secrecy between groups, our individual responsibilities as the SOJO design team didn't allow for much time to discuss the intricate details of each other's process. However, we did come to find out that one of the design teams was on the verge of not having a prepared proposal. Despite blocking it out of our collective consciousness, the "weak kitty in the litter" prophecy had come to fruition. Instead of SOJO, it was another school that was not selected during the proposal process. Setting off a scramble of potential suitors for the open slot, the presentations of the design teams became an interesting public spectacle moving toward final approval. Rito's reflections were important in terms of what the fourth school not making meant for the overall process.

> We fought against that (the weak kitty in the litter), but in the end we did not have four quality proposals . . . And it created a significant amount of issues with our young people actually coming together. One school had no structure of support. One of the principals was gone seven months later. Even when we finally came to realize that one of the four schools was not necessarily so good we said we actually should have opened three . . . politically the alderman wasn't going to allow that. He said we had to open four schools. We had to go with what the alderman said. That was significant. In the long run it actually hurt us. (Martinez interview, July 9, 2012)

The open proposal actually created a delay in the original schedule, as the design teams were supposed to get a planning year to hire teachers and align curriculum for CPS requirements. Ground had been broken for the school and construction was underway. From this moment (fall of 2004), there were less than ten months until opening day.

As word got out among the community of educators, organizers, and people who paid attention to local educational issues, a flood of potential suitors came for the open slot. Because the TAC was committed to an open process, each potential design team was required to present to the TAC. As public forums, many of the potential suitors would bring backers who were often vocal in the meetings. This made for quite the spectacle in that some of the design teams were unfamiliar with the community struggle and the values of the hunger strike. At one point this led to a series of protests in the open forums, as community members became vocal as to what school should be in the fourth slot. Although the TAC didn't approve them, one local charter network was contacted to give a presentation. Members were underwhelmed with their inability to answer questions in relationship to the community driven effort, in addition to explaining strict and draconian rules around discipline (students were fined in their demerits and were not allowed to graduate if the encumbrance was not paid) and achievement (the primary measure of academic performance was standardized tests scores). In the end, a second design team for the World Language school emerged and was subsequently approved by the TAC. The SOJO proposal, despite its challenges (particularly the budget, leadership, and curriculum components) secured TAC approval, approving Rito Martinez as the designated principal.

Even though he was approved as principal, CPS didn't provide for a salary in the planning year. Because of this major oversight by CPS officials, Rito had to use his pension from his former teaching position and personal savings to support himself until weeks before opening day. This was extremely taxing on him as the newly selected principal, but he decided to remain in the process despite the financial hardships.

Recruiting a Lead Teacher

One of the first hires Rito was able to make was for the lead teacher position.

At the time CPS had an enrollment requirement to have an assistant principal. Small schools, due their population (enrollment under six hundred students) were unable to hold an assistant principal salary as a budget line item. While not a full administrator, the lead teacher was a hybrid position that paired administrative responsibilities with reduced classroom instruction. When he first contacted his network of educators, many people were interested in the position. He wanted an experienced teacher who had the ability to take on administrative duties, particularly in planning an instructional support. Similar to his own financial challenges at the time, the people he originally targeted for the position were unable to take the substantial reduction in pay to make the job work for their current family situations.

Around the same time, he came in contact with Katherine "Katie" Hogan, an activist teacher who won a substantial battle against the city of Chicago in eliminating a CPS standardized exam. Known as the "Curie 12," they were able to eradicate the Chicago Academic Standards Examination (CASE) as part of the "Erase the CASE Campaign" (Hogan in Ayers et al. 2008, 97). They met through a mutual friend who was on the Math Science and Technology design team. In their conversations he alerted her that he was having a hard time filling the lead teacher position. After more efforts to get it filled, he asked her to interview for the position.

The interview went well and she accepted. However, the actual duties and responsibilities of the lead teacher were not well defined. By her account

> There was nothing written out for the lead teacher. We didn't really have a clear direction for what it meant for both of us to work together. We knew curriculum, we knew how to develop things to teach kids. Just didn't have a lot of training around

human resources, recruiting, interviewing . . . in the beginning we were just doing everything . . . It was exhausting and
exhilarating at the same time. Is was so exciting but we had no
idea. (Katie Hogan interview, July 17, 2012)

This exhaustion would revisit our process, but in the beginning many of us
were riding the wave of actually seeing things come together.

Developing/Hiring Staff

Once Katie was on, we were allowed to hire teaching faculty and staff.
Because SOJO would only have freshmen in the first year, there were a
reduced number of hires. CPS would guarantee new hires as needed, in
concert with the imminent population increases after year one. The hires
for the 2005–2006 school year were in English/reading/language arts, math,
art, music, social studies, science, physical education, Spanish, librarian,
two clerks, a social worker (Ana Herrera), and a special education resource
coordinator (Tiffany Ko).

Interviews were held between the LVCDC office and a CPS building that was a former K–8 school. Katie was interviewed at LVCDC. I
participated in the interviews for the English and math positions. Rico
Gutstein participated in and wrote questions for the math interviews. All
the interviews were by committee and included a sample lesson and questions regarding how they understood the concepts of social justice and its
relationship to their teaching.

In addition to being very intentional about going to see potential
teachers in their current positions, Rito was very strategic in making sure
that there was a combination of veteran and new teachers.

Half the staff had eight-years-plus experience and the other half
were new teachers. We couldn't have that with lump sum. I
would've hired all young folks with lump sum . . . that would
have hurt the process. (Martinez interview, July 9, 2012)

This allowed for a teacher "steal" in that we knew the best chance to get
the teachers we wanted would be to use our network of teachers that were
currently in classrooms. Despite the fact that there was great potential to
be turned down (as we were many times), this was the best place to start.
Knowing that veteran teachers have higher salaries, the core positions budget

equation discussed in the previous chapter allowed for us to have the mix of seasoned and new teachers. Additionally, we tried to get teacher representation from North Lawndale and La Villita. We had minimal success in this category in that there was one teacher in the original group that was born and raised in North Lawndale. However, of the original staff, there were two teachers who came to live in North Lawndale and La Villita, respectively.

One of the first year teachers, Ida Joyce Sia, had just finished her student teaching at Madero, a local school in La Villita. She was contacted by Rico after her interview and was alerted that she got the position as math teacher. At another interview with me, Rico, and Rito, I was able to give the good news to Angela Sangha (now Angela Sangha-Gadsden), whom I had as an undergraduate. I remember the yell she let out when I told her that she got the position. Things were slowly coming together.

To the "Nut!": Professional Development and Team Building

As a newly minted staff, we were able to use CHSRI funds to take the newly hired teaching staff to a professional development session at University of Massachusetts–Amherst. Sponsored by the Social Justice Concentration in the College of Education, we were accepted as members of their Summer Social Justice Institute. Patty Buenrostro also accompanied the group, as she would be supporting the math team with Rico. We stayed at the Black Walnut Inn, which would affectionately become nicknamed the "Nut" for our time at the institute. The time there was significant in that we were able to craft what became our core beliefs.

Truth and Transparency

We will practice honesty and authenticity in our communication and relationships with students, our community, peers, and ourselves.

Struggle and Sacrifice

Our struggle is against systems of power that have been historically used to deny, regulate, and prohibit access to the most basic human rights that should be granted freely to members of society regardless of race, class, gender, sexual orientation, or religious belief. We accept the reality that such struggle will require sacrifice from all involved.

Ownership and Agency

We will take responsibility as agents and catalysts of change to
expose the truth about the functions of power, work (unite) to
interrupt their operations, and operate as producers of power to
meet the needs of the Greater Lawndale community.

Collective and Community Power

Through collective community power, we commit to a conscious
effort to overcome the intended historical obstacles that have
been designed to disempower and divide our communities, and
thereby meet the needs of all members of Greater Lawndale
for continual betterment and progress. http://sj.lvlhs.org/apps/
pages/?uREC_ID=147999&type=d&pREC_ID=285138)

These were critical as faculty and staff experienced the growing pains of
being a new school. Because many of the teachers were already well established as the justice-centered teacher at their former institution, we needed
commonly agreed on goals. Having many of these people in the same place
created a different dynamic.

Everyone was the superstar at their old school. They were the
only ones that did social justice work at their school. Put all
those people together and it's a very different situation. We're
so used to working in isolation and being competitive with
other teachers that didn't agree with our pedagogy, so we had
to prove our classes were better. So now we're all together, we
had to totally switch our paradigm. And it takes a long working
relationship in order to do that. It's nothing personal, it just
takes a long time to figure out how someone else teaches and
how you can work together in a really good way. (Katie Hogan
interview, July 17, 2012)

When there were disputes, the core beliefs served as an important reference,
reminding teachers of the importance of their work.

Another development that came from the institute was the idea of
teacher introductions to families. Instead of referencing them as "home visits," the idea was completely the opposite. Though the visits were first met
with some trepidation, it was not the intent of the group to participate in
invasive, intrusive home visits reminiscent of a government department of

child and family services. On the contrary, the idea was to go to a student's house, introduce themselves as SOJO staff to the families, while giving them contact information if they had any questions about the school. Unless they were invited inside, the idea was for families to be able to associate a name with a face, to engender a sense of belonging if the parent for any reason had questions or needed to come to the school. This became an annual practice for the families of incoming freshmen. The idea of getting families familiar with staff before any problems arose was critical if there ever was an issue with a student.

Bringing things full circle, we met an excited undergraduate student by the name of Herman Shelton; because he was close to finishing his time as an undergraduate student and had heard about the school, he sought Rito out to find out more about SOJO. He heard about the school and looked Rito up specifically. They talked about a job he was taking in Chicago as one of the coordinators for the TRIO program at Roosevelt University. Over the years this would become a major resource for our students.

Authentic College Connections

Because SOJO is listed as a college prep school, we wanted to be explicit in establishing relationships with local universities. Rico and I were able to develop a relationship with our university (chapter 5), but there were other opportunities that afforded themselves to us during the design team process. One in particular came by way of Roosevelt University. As a local institution founded on the principles of social justice, a happenstance meeting between Rito and a Roosevelt University board member created a lasting relationship between both institutions.

At the same time, the circumstances of the meeting speak to the slippery slope between community-driven efforts and central office "requests." A CPS official from ONS asked if Rito would present at a donor's conference on Renaissance 2010. Despite the fact that SOJO was wrongly included in Renaissance 2010, Rito saw it as a potential opportunity to secure resources for the school. Although a highly dangerous play considering Chicago and CPS politics, it did secure a significant set of resources for the school. After his presentation, a vice president from the aerospace corporation Boeing approached Rito and said that she really liked what he was doing. She alerted him that she was on the Board of Trustees for Roosevelt University and wanted him to meet the president. She set up the meeting, and upon meeting with the president, he made a very bold promise to SOJO. He guaranteed a four-year scholarship to any student who graduated with 3.0 and a 20 on the ACT exam. He made this promise for the graduating classes of 2009 and 2010. Though many would see this as a huge victory for the school individually, the collective reality of Renaissance 2010 did not reap similar results for other schools throughout the city. While disinvestment and destabilization in other CPS schools is not the fault of SOJO, the neoliberal emphasis on the individual (school) obfuscates the systemic developments in other parts of the city. In this instance Renaissance 2010 appears advantageous for a few, while many continue to get more of the same. Fortunately, it didn't take us down the road of complete neoliberal corporate takeover in the life of the school.

In addition to the presidents' promise, he granted every incoming freshman class full access to the university. For the first six years we held freshman orientation on Roosevelt's campus, providing them access to college life early on and offering them a glimpse of what could be in store on graduating high school. From our earlier experiences at UMass Amherst with Herman (who was now TRIO coordinator at Roosevelt), we were able to bring the programs Upward Bound and College Bridge to SOJO.

Schedule

With our victories came an interesting set of compromises with CPS regarding our schedule. At the time nearing our opening, CPS had a policy for new high schools, under ONS. If 40 percent of the students scored in the lower quartile in reading and math, they would be required to take a double period of the subject. From this requirement we decided to go to a block schedule, with the same classes taking place on Monday, Wednesday, and Friday, and another set of courses on Tuesday and Thursday. By our assessment, this didn't work for teachers or students. The periods were too long compared to what everyone was used to. Additionally, the end of each block exhausted both teachers and students.

However, in year two we switched to a modified block schedule that was more conducive to teaching and learning. This allowed flexibility and allowed SOJO to coordinate with the bell schedule for the rest of the school.

Whereas items like a school schedule would appear to be mundane, scheduling can become a critical factor in establishing instructional culture in a school. With this in tow, Rito began to build up some capacity in dealing with CPS from a certain perspective. Instead of curtailing to the whims of the central office, the general rule for the central office was that the first answer to their suggestions should be "no."

> I quickly learned that . . . there's a fallacy that you can't say "no" to CPS. That was the premise of everything we did . . . we always said "no" . . . it was fine, as long as we came up with something that was intelligent and sound, they were fine with it, so I just carried that in to my principalship . . . I said "no" all the time but had a plan . . . I had a better plan and executed it on that total plan . . . and I think it's critical . . . whenever you're trying to do something different within the same power structure, you have to be able to say "no." You also have to deal with having those buttons . . . you are in the ecosystem of the beast . . . the last button was the community . . . and I knew that was the button you don't push until you know you gotta push . . . but we had different buttons. And saying "no" was the first button. (Martinez interview, July 9, 2012)

Unfortunately Rito's position is rare among principals. At the same time, repeatedly saying "no" may have ultimately had its time as the years progressed. As the school moved forward, we were slowly becoming known for our programming and academic achievement For whatever reason, in the fourth year of the school's existence, Rito was alerted that he would be removed from his post as principal because he was in violation of the residency requirement. Put in place by Richard J. Daley in the 1950s, the idea was to secure a tax base for the city by requiring teachers, principals, police officers, and firefighters to live in the city's boundaries. Where this is a sporadically enforced edict in Chicago (especially in CPS), someone in central office decided to enforce it in a subtle attempt to destabilize the school. Where we do not have the evidence that proves intent, the enforcement of the policy was dubious as best.

School Culture

The school is also deeply centered in ritual. The staff felt that this was critical in creating a positive school culture. For students and faculty to see that they were part of the same process, creating this culture came in the form of candle-lighting ceremonies, town hall meetings, and group social events that were centered on creating a sense of camaraderie. Using the work of Andrade and his rearticulation of the definite dozen from NCAA women's championship coach Pat Summit, his reconstructed set of her points resonated with the staff of SOJO.

To enter your revolutionary state of mind:

1. Be responsible (To yourself, your family, to your community to our world.)

2. Be respected, be respectful (Respect yourself. Demand that others respect you. Respect others.)

3. Be honest (Leaders don't make excuse, they make improvements.)

4. Be loyal (Stand alongside those who have the least.)

5. To discipline your revolutionary state of mind:

6. Work (Everyday, everywhere.)

7. Study (To study is a revolutionary duty.)

8. Character over reputation (Character is who you are when no one else is looking. Reputation is who other people say you are.)

9. Believe (Doubters never win, revolutionaries never doubt.)

10. To build a successful revolution:

11. Be self-critical (No revolution is complete without a culture of self-improvement. There is no culture of self-improvement without a culture of self-reflection.)

12. Acknowledge the knowledge (Teach and be teachable.)

13. Build with allies; Influence the enemy (Execute the 5 phases: identify, analyze, plan, implement, evaluate.)

14. Be relentless (Never, ever give up.) (Duncan Andrade, 2010)

From these points, SOJO staff (facilitated by Troy Kamau LaRaviere), developed the Essential 7. Every semester and at every graduation there is an awards ceremony where students are presented with awards associated with each of the following values.

1. Unity: We must struggle together as sisters and brothers or perish together as fools.

2. Respect: True strength is always based on love, care, and respect for yourself and others. Disrespect is a weak person's imitation of strength.

3. Self Discipline: If you discipline yourself, no one else will have to.

4. Excellence: We must make an extraordinary effort in order to become extraordinary students, extraordinary teachers, and an extraordinary school.

5. Service: We will make ourselves better people by working to make life better for other human beings.

6. Honesty & Ownership: If your words and actions match, you will gain trust and respect. So, we will not make excuses, we will make improvements.

7. Being Prompt & Prepared: We must come on time and we must come ready. We cannot make our shield and spear in the middle of the battlefield.

The idea is to create an ethos where students and faculty understand what's trying to be done at the school. It exists with contradictions, but to have them in the daily understandings of the school has been key in times of internal and external conflict.

Early Student Engagement

Now that one of the most expensive school buildings to be built in the state of Illinois was open, there had to be the business of implementing the curriculum that was planned. In our first year, we had a couple of instances that challenged us to engage concepts of social justice. Some were returning to the issue brought forward as concerns from members of the TAC, while others were age-old concerns germane to life in Chicago.

Reigniting an issue of concern, it had come to the attention of SOJO faculty and administration that Martin Sandoval, the elected state senator from La Villita, wanted to pass an ordinance reconfiguring the boundaries to keep residents from North Lawndale out of the multiplex. Framed as making the school accessible to more members of La Villita, passage of the proposed ordinance would have devastating effects for students from North Lawndale. Leaning on the idea that he had the overwhelming support of his constituents on the issue, he also publically called for Rito's resignation as SOJO principal. Once the staff found out about the conflict, one of the math teachers (Phi Pham) encouraged the Math Department to teach a unit on demography and proportions. Rico remembers the moment as pivotal in the development of some of the new teachers.

> When Sandoval came out with the boundaries madness, Phi came out and said that we have to teach this. She understood that it was a teachable moment and pushed. Mathematically it wasn't so wonderful but the fact that it was a real question that we jumped on. That synthesized the 3 Cs because it came straight from the question: What is a fair solution for both communities? Students were extremely invested and people argued the proportions (e.g., should it be 70/30, 45/55, etc.). There was a lot of math being done. That was a good example of what we were trying to do. (Gutstein interview, July 30, 2012)

In addition to the mathematics lesson, students wrote letters to Sandoval explaining what they were doing in math class and how his efforts to exclude North Lawndale were not in concert with what the school was created to do. Coupled with the reignited efforts of LVCDC and LCDC, Sandoval's referendum was defeated and students got a taste of the potential for community coalitions from both communities.

Another moment came in the form of transportation. During the first semester, African-American students were being accosted on Thirty-First Street between Pulaski and Kostner. This stretch of land became quite notorious for conflict, especially since African-American students were instantly associated with a rival neighborhood with or without particular gang/street organization affiliations.

This prompted members of the English Department to engage on issues of what constitutes justice in this instance. Students were given a writing assignment to address the Chicago Transit Authority (CTA) on the issue. Some students suggested a bus route that traveled down Thirty-First Street. From a partnership with a local community organization (Little Village Environmental Justice Organization, LVEJO), students discovered that there used to be a bus line that serviced Thirty-First Street that had been discontinued.

Upon their discovery, teachers and students agreed that action steps should be taken. Since the assignment was centered in finding viable solutions to real world problems, students made the suggestion to present their issues to the Chicago Transit Board (the governing body of CTA). On June 14, 2006, a group of freshmen from the reading class prepared a statement and presented it to the board. The first response from the board was, "Who are your teachers?" Upon hearing this question, the students pointed to the back of the room where we were standing, and continued to congratulated students for being so "articulate" and well-spoken. Paternalism aside, students were provided with temporary relief in the form of a temporary bus service that would pick students up from the front doors of the building and give them rides to Pulaski. Originally, the bus service appeared to be a substantial victory. Unfortunately the service was canceled due to budget cuts in CTA.

As colloquium was getting off the ground, some teachers heavily resonated with the idea of creating topics that students would self-select. I had the opportunity to team-teach my colloquium with a law student, giving students the opportunity to investigate issues that were important to their lives with regard to the law. I had the opportunity to teach a video documentation class two years later in a colloquium that produced a video, which was shown to the entire student body as an investigation of issues in the neighborhood.

Revisiting an age-old issue, students became very aware of race. African-American students began to express how they felt as if they were unwanted at the school and wanted to leave. In some cases, this led to students lashing out against each other in the hallways and in the lunchroom. Upon getting word of this, the SOJO staff began a series of race dialogues with each other and students about how the school was born out of a struggle to put the communities together. Over the years, the Essential 7 became critical in threading through the school culture with constant reminders of the intentions of the school. All of these experiences gave me enough to move into teaching my own course.

Chapter 5

Educational Debt Relief

Classroom Struggles, Critical Race Praxis, and the Politics of School

In her 2006 presidential address to the American Educational Research Association, Gloria Ladson-Billings posed a challenge to researchers, classroom educators, community organizers, and students to rethink the concept of the "achievement gap." Reframing the issue as one of an "educational debt," Ladson-Billings challenges members of the aforementioned groups to critique the language of the gap to address the historical lineage of exclusion and resistance in urban areas. In simple terms, the educational debt is "the forgone schooling resources that we could have (should have) been investing in (primarily) low income students" (Haveman in Ladson-Billings, 2006). Instead of thinking about the "gap" as a description of the achievement disparity between students of color and their White counterparts, Ladson-Billings suggests that we think of our teaching and engaged scholarship as paying a debt that is owed to students and families in light of the historical resource disparities that have plagued urban schools, primarily populated by low-income African-American and Latino/a youth. One particular passage made her concept clear in terms of how our course should be positioned.

> . . . we must use our imaginations to construct a set of images that illustrate the debt. The images should remind us that the cumulative effect of poor education, poor housing, poor health care, and poor government services create a bifurcated society that leaves more than children behind. The images should compel us to deploy our knowledge, skills, and expertise to alleviate the suffering of the least of these. (Ladson-Billings 2006, 10)

Upon reading her remarks, I began to rethink the purpose of policies under the Bush and Obama administrations positioned the purpose of federal legislation like the Troubled Asset Relief Fund and the American Reinvestment and Relief Act. Because the educational policies of No Child Left Behind and Race to the Top are not aimed at improving the education of the masses, a reimagining needs to take place (Leonardo 2009). This such reimagining moves away from job growth stimulation and supporting corporate banking institutions that were "too big to fail," to addressing the debt incurred for the legacy of disinvestment and marginalization in Black and Brown communities. For myself, our students were "too valuable to be ignored."

For the remainder of this chapter, the concept of educational debt is directly coupled with the tenets of CRT and CRP. From CRT, the "commitment to social justice" is critical, as the "justice" condition in this project is access to colleges and universities. From CRP, the course was specific to the performative, material, and reflexive tenets. To incorporate the performative, the course was indicative of the tangible actions steps needed to address the issue at hand (lack of college access). The material tenet was evidenced in our charge to develop a project that would address the lack of college access by reviving a dormant institutional structure rarely available to working-class/low-income Black and Latino/a youth. By the end of the class, we needed to incorporate the reflexive element in order to revisit our theoretical understandings based on the practical, real life events that took place in our classroom.

Mentioned in chapter 4, the proposal for SOJO contained language stating the intent of two college professors (me and Eric "Rico" Gutstein) to teach at the high school, with the goal of providing early college access to our students. As members of the design team, during the first three years of the high school (2005–2008), Rico and I worked with faculty and students in math and social studies, respectively. Our duties and responsibilities rested primarily in the capacity of developing curriculum, coteaching and modeling lessons for the faculty. As the students who began as freshmen at SOJO in the fall of 2005 approached their senior year, Rico and I, along with SOJO faculty and administration, returned to the original idea in the proposal, stating that we would create classes for SOJO seniors, providing them with dual (high school and college) credit for completion of the course. Confronted with the practical realities of coordinating high school and college schedules, we thought the best way to provide the course would be for us to teach the classes on-site at SOJO.

Trying to Make it Work: Putting Theory to the Test

While developing the proposal for SOJO, one of the components to the document was a section stating my and Rico's intent to teach at the high school, in order to provide college access to students traditionally excluded from this opportunity. In Rico's case, his work led to student presentations at numerous research and teaching conferences, while my work culminated in a number of presentations during the year that students participated in the college bridge course. As the students who began at SOJO in the fall of 2005 approached their senior year, Rico and I, along with SOJO faculty and administration, began to discuss the possibilities of students attaining early college credit. Utilizing our networks as university professors, we were able to contact the university while the SOJO administration addressed our concerns with CPS.

During this time officials at our local university alerted us that they currently offered a college bridge program on campus. They wanted to revitalize the program in that it was virtually dormant with fewer than ten students throughout the entire university. However, because they had established a partnership with CPS, we figured that we could place our students into their existing structure. Similar to college bridge programs across the country, students at our local university would be enrolled in an actual university course, taking the class on the campus with other college students. Although this sounded optimal, we presented it to SOJO's administration. The idea sounded good in theory, but SOJO administration forewarned us of potential scheduling conflicts, specifically concerning transportation between SOJO and the university. With the support of the assistant principal, we tried to develop an adjustment to the traditional lecture-discussion-style college course. The original idea had students taking our courses at the university, while participating in a discussion section that would take place at the high school. Essentially, students would take our classes for two days at the university, receiving an early dismissal from SOJO on the days they would have classes with us. The other three days during the week, students would take a discussion section at the high school at the same time they would have the university course. My course would be called Education, Youth, and Justice, while Rico's course would be called Using Mathematics to Write the World. The third course would be an English course that would meet most general education requirements at most four-year universities.

Despite our original idea, scheduling presented several issues. The fact that SOJO offered three college bridge courses during the 2008–2009 school year meant that seniors could potentially rotate between SOJO and the university up to four times in a week. With a small student body (less than four hundred students) and staff (twenty-five teachers, two counselors, one social worker, two office staff, and three administrators at the time), the proposed schedule would be impossible. Because we develop student schedules in the beginning of the academic year, we wouldn't be able to coordinate students leaving campus and returning numerous times in the day. Additionally, SOJO is a little less than eight miles from the university and is not easily accessible by public transportation. Confronted with these realities, we thought the best way to provide the courses would be to teach the classes on-site at SOJO. This would include us being on campus five days per week, one period per day, with the addition of any time we used to update the administration on the progress of the course. The course would be the equivalent of two semesters long, in that it ran for the entire school year at SOJO. I received a real challenge in that my class was scheduled for first period (8 a.m.).

Upon discussing this idea, we became excited about the possibilities of teaching a college course on a high school campus. The professor who taught the third course was on board with the arrangement. For my course, I also had a research assistant, who would attend class during the session while teaching some units if I had any absences due to travel. Our work would be in concert with the likes of Majors (2010), Hill (2009), Lee and Majors (2003), Duncan-Andrade and Morrell (2008), Camangian (2011), Cammarota (2014), and Yang (with Tuck 2012), all of whom are university professors who have taught high school courses while holding positions as university faculty. With my class in particular, my personal interactions with the aforementioned authors were influential in positioning the course. Remaining accountable to the community-driven initiative, our decision to teach the class on campus allowed for a more tangible connection to the intent of the initial proposal for SOJO.

Despite confidence in our version of the program with the university, we were hit with yet another roadblock in terms of a grade point average (GPA) requirement. Because many traditional college bridge programs are reserved for high-achieving students, we had to make adjustments for our students who did not have the required 3.0 GPA. To resolve the situation, Rico and I wrote letters of recommendation for the students who didn't meet the GPA requirement. Fortunately for us, all of the students we wrote the letters for were allowed to take the class. Whereas this roadblock was minor, we knew CPS presented another set of challenges.

Because the principal had some insights as to what CPS's concerns would be, he arranged a meeting at the CPS central office building. There we met with the CPS official responsible for postsecondary education. As is the case with many central office administrators, his initial concerns were around the areas of budget, as our students would be required to pay tuition fees for the courses. When we assured him of our university's commitment to the college innovation we proposed, he alerted us that he felt that central office would be amenable to the suggested changes, as long as we could make them fit in the schedule. In terms of tuition, the university and CPS decided to split the costs. This was extremely beneficial to us in that it is unusual for central office to provide tuition funds for bridge programs.

The Course: Education, Youth, and Justice

My course was titled Education, Youth, and Justice (ED-196), in reference to the work communities of color have engaged in to demand justice in education from a critical historical, political, and contemporary perspective. Pairing concepts of social justice with current and historical interpretations of youth culture, one of the objectives of the course was to apply interpretations of social justice to analyze urban public education. In Chicago (and in other cities across the United States), because many students, families, and community members are in an epic battle to save their schools and homes, investigating the different perspectives of justice allowed for rich inquiry and exchange. Even with the advent of SOJO as a new school, students understood how the intended purpose of the community-driven initiative that led to the high school could be hijacked under the false guise of "development." To make the idea tangible, for my course it was important to delineate the current mainstream positioning of social justice education. Returning to my earlier frustrations stated in the introduction around the concept, the idea was to frame the course around the ways in which justice has been conceptualized locally and internationally. The hope was to engage in a form of justice-centered education that was explicit in foregrounding the investigation of what justice means to the students taking the course. From this idea, all of the assignments required students to articulate the "justice" condition to issues they find relevant to their lives.

As engaged scholarship, the attempt was to model our work in the mold of the aforementioned scholars who've taught high school courses while holding positions as university faculty. By investigating, documenting, and analyzing success and conflict in the communities of North Lawndale and La Villita, one of the course's stated goals was to provide insight into how resolutions are made across issues of race, class, and power through implementation of a college-access program for African-American and Latino/a youth.

Materials for the course included four books, student journals, and a course packet. Supplemental materials (handouts, poster boards, markers, video cameras, etc.) were used as needed, depending on the research projects of the students. In framing education broadly, one of the books (Howard Zinn's *On Democratic Education*) and the course packet contained articles that specifically addressed K–16 education. In addition to education-specific content, the packet also contained a section on youth and community organizing. For the purposes of the course, justice-centered education is understood as the process by which people are able to ask critical questions while making informed decisions centered in improving the human condition at the individual and collective level. The second text, Vijay Prashad's *The Darker Nations*, uses critical historiography to highlight justice movements of people of color throughout the world. The last two texts investigated the philosophy of race (Charles Mills's *The Racial Contract*) and legal scholarship (Richard Delgado and Jean Stefancic's *Critical Race Theory: An Introduction*). All of the texts were critical in developing the course.

A Good Teacher Is a Good Thief: Pushing for Relevant Curriculum

A comrade always reminds me of how we often mistakenly think of justice-centered, relevant teaching as a solitary act. Instead, he is quick to state that our work is often collectively imagined and executed. From this point he always jokes that a "good teacher is a good thief." In our conversations he always reminds me that if you see something you think will work in your class, it is your responsibility to "steal" it. Not in the literal sense, but "stealing" as figurative language reflecting the urgency of the moment in the education of Black and Latino/a youth. Because the justice condition requires the acknowledgment of the source of our work, processes, and actions, we should always give credit to the creator of the actions we incorporate. In too many instances, both in academia and K–12 education, the originators of concepts are not given proper credit, strengthening the stranglehold of the colonial project in education.

Similar to the work discussed in chapter 3, it became critically impor-tant for me to utilize my various networks to develop activities and units for the course. Two of the main sources that I would borrow from would be the Institute for Democracy, Education, and Access (IDEA) at the University of California, Los Angeles, and the Step to College Program (STC) of San Francisco State University. I first had the opportunity to observe and talk with members of IDEA in the summer of 2004, as they were establishing their summer research institute and the teacher inquiry project. In both projects, what became clear to me was the idea that relevant curriculum can be developed through the process of familiarizing students with research methodology and theory. Oakes and Rogers (2006) discuss the development of the IDEA Summer Research Institute, developed to engage high school youth with university-level research and analysis. As an amalgamation of the observations and conversations with numerous educators across the country who take a justice-centered approach to education, the hope of the course was to engage theory and research on the ground with students.

As a University of California Presidential Postdoctoral Scholar, Jeffrey Duncan-Andrade worked with IDEA in developing the Summer Research Institute and the Teacher Inquiry Project. Along with then–faculty member Ernest Morrell, students were taken from all parts of Los Angeles to engage in projects that investigated the conditions of their schools and neighborhoods. Upon leaving IDEA for a faculty position at San Francisco State University (SFSU), he coupled his efforts with the Step to College Program, already a fixture at the university since 1986. By pairing his efforts with STC, he was able to use the infrastructure of SFSU to support his work at East Oakland Community High School (EOC). Also discussed in chapter 3, in addition to the development of the proposal from the design team, EOC was also influential in the development of the Education, Youth, and Justice class.

Unique to his iteration of STC, Andrade and K. Wayne Yang (another cofounder of EOC) developed a course that took a group of freshmen in 2004 through their senior year, granting them access to college courses and college professors. Over the four years this group of students presented at national and international academic conferences, citing their use of qualita-tive methodology and critical analysis (Duncan-Andrade, 2009). Through my observation of the EOC/STC partnership, I was able to engage in con-versations with Duncan-Andrade and Yang about ways in which to develop curriculum for the class, centering the lessons and units in critical analysis. The challenge, however, was to fit what they did in four years in the span of one academic school year.

Another program that was deeply influential to the development of the course was the Raza Studies Program of the Tucson Unified School District (TUSD). My first observations of the project came at a meeting of the American Educational Research Association (AERA) meeting in 2004. During their presentation at the meeting, then-director Augustine Romero and University of Arizona Mexican-American Studies professor Julio Cammarota discussed a program called the Social Justice Education Project (SJEP). Similar to IDEA and STC, the idea was to incorporate critical analysis to the study of school conditions throughout TUSD. The presentation was informative and inspirational, as the student presenters were articulate and explicit with the needs of Mexican-American students throughout Tucson. I was introduced to Romero and Cammarota through Duncan-Andrade, which brought me to meet Raza Studies Educators Curtis Acosta, Jose Gonzalez, Norma Gonzalez, Maria Brummer, Sean Arce, Rene Martinez, Sally Rusk, Lorenzo Lopez, and Alexandro Escamilla. Documented extensively in film and text, the struggles of the Raza Studies Program allowed me to recognize the centrality of human relationships in the development of relevant curriculum (Cammarota and Fine 2010, Cammarota, Romero, & Arce 2009, Cammarota & Romero 2014). Despite the program being dismantled by the Arizona Legislature in 2012, its lasting effects resonate throughout the country and continue to serve as testament to the possibilities of thoughtful, justice-centered education.

Pairing the 3 Cs with IRPIE

All of the aforementioned programs utilized Freirean concepts in their development and implementation. Duncan-Andrade and Morell (2008) include their interpretation of Freirean analysis in their cycle of critical praxis. The process of identifying, researching, planning, implementing, and evaluating (IRPIE, "eye are pie") were critical in creating student-generated projects aimed at addressing an issue students found important to their lives. Cammarota, Romero, and Arce utilized a similar process to create what they describe as a "critically compassionate Barrio Pedagogy" (Cammarota, Romero, & Arce, 2009). Both concepts were critical in that they allowed me to develop incorporate concepts centered in inquiry, over irrelevant state mandates.

To center this as skill development for qualitative research, it became important to pair the 3 Cs with the cycle of critical praxis. Because they had familiarized themselves with the 3 Cs in other courses, the pairing of the constructs came in the form of students articulating what "C" was addressed in each component of IRPIE. In order to begin this journey one of our first units focused on an issue I mistakenly thought to be centrally relevant to the majority of my students in the course.

Hip-Hop, Urban Renewal, and Gentrification

In creating this unit, I felt one of the best ways to connect the current contexts of young people to the foundation of hip-hop was to provide an analysis of urban renewal/gentrification. Chicago youth, while not always articulating the moniker "gentrification," are very familiar with the process through personal or family experiences. With my students, some were in the process of moving or had family members who relocated to suburbs for available housing. Drawing a parallel to the situation of the South Bronx of the 1970s, I felt that students would make tangible sense of the concept through the study of hip-hop.

It should be noted, however, that not all of my students were avid fans of hip-hop. Whereas some felt themselves to be deeply engrained in the culture of hip-hop, other students were fans of Mexican Kumbia, R&B, country and western, and speed metal. Hip-hop, however, provided a point of entry in that they were minimally familiar with it, in terms of media (TV and radio), music, and culture. Their familiarity, however minimal, allowed us to enter the primary text for the unit.

Where Chicago is in the midst of a forty-plus-year wave of uneven development/gentrification, the parallels to New York City are evident. To contextualize this reality, we used chapter 1 of Jeff Chang's *Can't Stop Won't Stop* to provide a social, political, and economic context for hip-hop. The provocative title of the chapter ("Necropolis") allowed the class to engage in some lively discussion around what we would consider to be a "city of death." When I asked students to describe what a necropolis could be, they talked about a place that was infested with drugs, high crime, poverty, and few social services. I continued to probe that if they thought there were any necropolises that they knew about. A few students responded, "We could say that about some parts of Chicago." As others nodded their heads some chimed in that Chicago is more complex than that. When I asked them to speak to the complexities, they returned that there are a number of experiences in Chicago that would allow us to consider it a necropolis, while to others it could still be a city of dreams. I asked them whom Chicago would be a city of dreams for. Some students said that it would be that way for the folks who were gentrifying the city. Others thought that it would be a city of dreams for families who immigrated to the city to make a better life for their families.

If students could grasp how Chicago could be considered as a city of death to some, I felt that we could smoothly transition into Chang's interpretation of New York City as a necropolis. Chang leads readers into the setting of the necropolis through a discussion of White flight and insurance arson, beginning with the 1977 baseball World Series. As the people who could not move out of the city were largely African-American and Caribbean (mostly Puerto Rican and Jamaican), hip-hop became the instrument by which young people were able to respond to their conditions. With the construction of the Cross Bronx Expressway, the residents who remained after the razing of property were largely poor and were unable to relocate. Coupled with the removal of music and art programs in New York City Public Schools, hip-hop, through DJing, MCing, graffiti, and breakdancing, became the musical and physical expression by which young people were able to respond to the conditions in the South Bronx. This resonated with my students in that they saw what young people at that time were creating in response to gentrification. There was a historical connection to Chicago in that the 1977 City of New York report called "The South Bronx: A Plan for Revitalization" acknowledged that the damage done to the South Bronx "could not be measured in numbers" (Chang 2005, 17). In Chicago, some six years earlier, a plan called the "Chicago 21" was created that identified twenty-one geographic and political wards as sites that were beyond repair and needed to be "revitalized." Because urban planning policies of the seventies were steeped in the language of urban renewal, students were able to identify the connection to gentrification in Chicago. As the city of New York made a concerted effort to "remove" residents who were deemed disposable, a similar plan was in place in Chicago. Coupled with the economic downturn, disinvestment in public infrastructure and services (transportation, streets, and sanitation services; education, state, and federal employment programs), New York City (and urban cities throughout the country) found itself in a major crisis. Instead of reaching its desired outcome of moving African-American and Latino/a residents out of the five boroughs, the move resulted in the reconcentration of poverty.

The historical realities of urban renewal/gentrification in New York City resonated with my students in Chicago for several reasons. The neighborhoods that they come from (North Lawndale and Little Village) are witnessing the effects of a massive gentrification project. As one neighborhood is densely populated (Little Village), North Lawndale has the highest number of vacant lots in the city. Over the last ten years, rents have doubled on some blocks and property taxes have tripled in some areas of North Lawndale. Similar to the Cross Bronx Expressway in New York City, Ogden Avenue, which cuts through North Lawndale and Little Village, provides direct access to downtown and the central business district in Chicago. Because property along Ogden has been identified as desirable, developers have targeted vacant lots in North Lawndale for high-end condominium and single-family homes. At SOJO, this has resulted in students having to change addresses up to three or four times while new residents move to the area. Where Little Village and North Lawndale provide one context, it should be considered part of a larger plan to move residents who have been deemed "undesirable" out of the city. Similar to the conditions in New York, these "undesirable" populations continue to consist mainly of low-income/working-class African-American and Latino/a residents.

Returning to hip-hop, I had the students write a reflection on responses to gentrification. Because many students in this class were activists in their own right (many of the students in the class participated in developing policy initiatives, conference presentations, and curriculum development addressing police brutality, predatory lending, and standardized testing), I was familiar with their ability to synthesize information and develop an argument. In my own reflections, I wondered whether or not they saw any connection between the responses of African-American and Puerto Rican youth of the South Bronx in the 1970s and what was happening currently in Chicago. To my surprise, when I first posed the question, there was a lot of dead silence. Many of the students responded with confused looks. When I began to ask them to recall the conditions in the South Bronx, they began to pepper me with the information they read in Chang's chapter. I continued by asking them to talk about gentrification in Chicago, and they responded with information they had given me earlier in class. From there I asked them to connect the two and to write it down in a reflection. Once they made the connection, they were able to engage the writing exercise.

The reflection prompt contained two questions. First, why do you feel hip-hop was the response of young people to urban renewal/gentrification in New York City in the 1970s? Second, what is your creative response as a young person to urban renewal/gentrification in Chicago? Where the first question may be read as a reiteration of the earlier discussion, I wanted to focus on the second prompt, as it would signal the students' ability to analyze and process information to develop a cogent argument. Many of them felt their activism was the creative response, while others thought their connection to visual arts could be considered a creative form of resistance similar to hip-hop. One of my students is a painter and sculptor, while another is an avid guitarist who dedicates much of his time to composing music. Both felt that attending a social justice high school allowed them to hone their creative skills as visual and performing artists to address issues of injustice in their communities.

In understanding hip-hop in part as a response to urban renewal/gentrification, I often wonder what will be the next creative response of young people to conditions they determine to be unjust. When I asked my students, some shrugged their shoulders, while others felt it would be their activism around specific issues; yet others felt as if the answer was still in the works. Nevertheless, we agreed that hip-hop, in its original conception, should be considered another creative response to injustice and oppression. Their comments, while true to their experiences, were interesting for me to hear in that they provided me with perspective on some tangible disconnects between my perspective and their own.

Where I am no longer eighteen years old, I have to remember that there are some experiences that we share and also places where our experiences diverge. This especially becomes important in hip-hop, because some of my students and myself would identify with hip-hop as pivotal in our upbringing. Instead of viewing this as a "generational gap," I understand it as the recognition that there are many things that are different for my students than they were for me when I was the same age. In recognition of those differences, the challenge is to discover ways in which each of our experiences can inform the other in the larger quest for justice in education. Even with the reality that many of our experiences are different, many are the same or similar. The major difference, however, often lie in the intensity in which young people of color are persecuted and vilified. For example, where the issue of police brutality has consistently been an issue in working-class/low-income African-American and Latino/a communities, urban police forces have militarized themselves in light of a perceived "threat" in these areas. In Chicago, there was recently a proposed ordinance to arm every Chicago Police Department (CPD) squad car with M-4 assault rifles, which are designed to penetrate tank armor. Nevertheless, the music served as the necessary entry point by which to engage an example of how hip-hop, in many instances, was a response to the political, economic, and social conditions of the late seventies and early eighties. Just like early hip-hop provided context for me, I was making the attempt to provide context for them. Now understood as culturally relevant or culturally relevant teaching, my attempt was to use the views, values, opinions, and culture of young people as a portal by which to develop analytical and concrete skills (Ladson-Billings, 1994).

A Twenty-Eight-Person Article

One of the units for the course was inspired by an e-mail I received from an independent publisher soliciting articles about social justice in education. Upon pondering the request, I thought of Derrick Bell's work with his law students at New York University. As a graduate student, I was amazed that he wrote one article with his entire class. In thinking about ED 196, I thought about doing the same thing, except Bell's class had twelve students. Our class had twenty-seven.

Considering the challenge that publishing an article with twenty-eight authors would be, I brought the request to class to see if they were interested. Because it's often difficult to gage a group of seventeen- and eighteen-year-olds at eight o'clock in the morning, I wasn't sure as to how they would respond. In the end, I thought that it wouldn't hurt to give it a try. When I passed out the call for articles, my "sell" to the class was that their work would be published in a journal that's distributed across the country. To my surprise, they were really excited about the opportunity to publish the article.

Now that they decided to commit the work, the issue was to contact the publisher to see if something like this was possible. To get the ball rolling, I sent the journal editor an e-mail explaining the idea of publishing an article with twenty-eight authors. Again, to my amazement, she responded by saying that she was really excited about the idea, and looked forward to our submission. The challenge would be to capture the sentiments of twenty-seven students in less than fifteen hundred words. I volunteered to be the contact person for the editor, also with the challenge of delivering copy edits to be reviewed by class for the final edits.

The first issue with creating an article in this mode is figuring out a way to make sure that all of the students voices are accounted for. The best way to assure this was to divide the students into groups, selecting what portion of the course they wanted to speak to in the article. During this discussion, we decided to divide students into groups that were responsible for a particular section. One group decided to provide a definition of social justice. ED 196 was the topic for one of the groups. Another group decided to do a section on conflict. The last group decided to conclude the article, speaking to the importance of social justice in classes at SOJO (Stovall et al. 2009, 13).

With respect to the deadline, our goal was to finish two weeks before the due date, giving us time to finish and agree on the edits. Once students decided on their groups, to their credit, they were very diligent in finishing their paragraphs on time.

Once the paragraphs were compiled, I copyedited the set, only checking for spelling errors and sentence continuity. I passed the article back to the students for final edits, their responsibility being to make sure the essence of the article was maintained and the spirit of their writing was not compromised. As a group, they offered their edits in class and felt the work was ready for submission. Once we sent it off to the editor, she thanked us for our work. Instead of having to pay for twenty-eight copies of the journal, she was gracious enough to donate copies to the class, making sure that every student had a copy of his or her work. As this served as our entry to sharing our critical analysis in the public sphere, the next unit sought to intensify our analysis.

The Racial Contract

Charles Mills, in his seminal reframing of the social contract offered by Enlightenment philosophers Locke and Hume, argues that the social contract is inefficient in explaining the current conditions of people of color in the Western Hemisphere.

> What is needed is a global theoretical framework for situating discussions of race and White racism, and thereby challenging the assumptions of White political philosophy, which would correspond to feminist theorists' articulation of the centrality of gender, patriarchy, and sexism to traditional moral and political theory. What is needed, in other words, is a recognition that racism . . . is *itself* a political system, a particular power structure of formal or informal rule, socioeconomic privilege, and norms for the differential distribution of material wealth and opportunities, benefits and burdens, rights and duties. (Mills 1997, 2–3)

The "contract," is a signed one, in the sense that life for people of color in the Western Hemisphere is reflective of a set of decisions that operate on the premise of dehumanization. If people are dehumanized or thought of as less than human, the laws that govern the land concretize the idea, often resulting in further marginalization and isolation. An example I used repeatedly in the class was the example of the clause of the Thirteenth Amendment of the U.S. Constitution, stating that slavery is thereby abolished except for instances of "involuntary servitude" for punishment. Currently, because these instances of involuntary servitude are now completely relegated to the prison industrial complex (PIC) by way of mass incarceration, the example of the Thirteenth Amendment becomes sanguine in explaining the concept of the contract.

Because my class was familiar with the Thirteenth Amendment example, the idea was to deepen the concept of the contract. To begin, I started with the definition of a contract: An agreement between two or more parties for the doing or not doing of something specified.

Because the definition is pretty straightforward, students were able to generate examples of contracts, ranging from mortgages, cellular phone service providers, to recording contracts. From these examples, I distributed copies of an actual cell phone provider. Upon reading through the legalese of the contract, I had students focus on the last paragraph, which happened to be in fine print. Paraphrasing the language of the contract, the document states that if there was a dispute with the company for more than $6,000, the signee of the contract could not engage in a lawsuit. Everyone in the class found this language to be strange for a contract, but in concert with the definition of a contract: an agreement for the doing or not doing of something. In this instance signing meant you could not file suit.

This allowed us to move into our larger researcher assignment: *to use the cycle of critical praxis to explain how the racial contract affects one or more of the nine areas of human life and activity* (education, economics, entertainment, labor, law, religion, sex [gender], war and politics). In addition to an individual research paper, students were also required to develop a public presentation to be presented to a group of researchers at a local university. We also invited Professor Mills to the presentation. The idea was to get students to develop an assignment similar to the ones students would get in college.

Once students began to grapple with the idea of a racial contract existing in the United States, some of the chosen topics were immigration, gentrification, school discipline policies for LGBTQ youth of color, reproductive rights, and health care. In the same way that I supervise research projects for my undergraduate and graduate students, my main role was to serve in a support role. From their topics, I would provide additional resources while contacting people in my network of schools, organizations, and researchers to secure relevant information for their research assignments.

Bringing It All Back Home

As promised, we secured a day and time to present to researchers at a local university. Unfortunately, due to previous travel arrangements, Professor Mills was unable to attend but let the class know how honored he was that they were using his text to analyze their conditions. Some of the students expressed their nervousness as we approached the university, but I told them not to worry, they were well-prepared and would not have a problem in their presentations. Earlier in the week, with the help of clerical staff, I was able to publicize the event in several departments throughout the College of Education and the College of Liberal Arts and Sciences. The event was well attended by university faculty and staff. Also in attendance was the associate dean who was instrumental in providing the initial matching funds for tuition and supplies for the students.

I provided a brief introduction of the course and explained how Rico and I were engaging in a yearlong project to provide high school students with early college entrance credit. From there students began to present their group presentations on the Racial Contract. From explaining the premise of the text, they began to explain gentrification, immigration, and health care. Followed by a question-and-answer session, faculty asked students on how they came to their projects and what were their key discoveries. Students responded soundly to the questions, providing definitive answers that were situated in their research. Many of my fellow colleagues approached me after the presentation, congratulating me and the students on the projects.

In debriefing with the students, they admitted that they were nervous at first, but began to feel comfortable as they got into their presentation. They also said they felt prepared to address questions because of the time they spent working on the project. The idea of fully immersing themselves in the work allowed them to understand their topic from a number of perspectives. Despite my feeling of pride in the presentations, there was still work to do.

The Unit

The last component of the class was something that is often discussed as "overstanding." Often a colloquialism used in African-American and Carribean Christian traditions, the concept usually denotes the ability to demonstrate understanding of a concept or idea by the ability to teach it. Discussed in the beginning of the class, the idea was for students to develop a curriculum unit that would be taught to incoming freshmen the following year. In order to develop the unit, we used the same rubric currently used by SOJO teachers in addition to the 3 Cs. As part of the assignment, each unit was required to include an overview, objectives, relevant disciplines, materials, key terms, activities/assignments, and assessments. We promised that these units would be used as the baseline to create units for a freshmen history course.

Again, students began with their interests, developing curricular units ranging from deportations, organ trafficking, blood diamonds, and the connection between the environment at historical research. In the attempt to develop a sense of ownership in students, creation of the curricular units served as a tangible example of students contributing to the future of the school. In developing the unit, I asked students to consider either what they enjoyed the most in their experience at SOJO or something they would have liked to have studied while they were in high school. To this day, some of the concepts discussed in the curricular units are still used in the freshmen world studies course, especially on issues of environment, race, and cities (they study the 1995 Chicago heat wave through the work of sociologist Eric Klinenberg (2004) and ornithologist Jared Diamond's *Guns, Germs, and Steel*) (1997).

Reflexivity and CRP: Unpacking the Disconnects and Contradictions for Liberation

Throughout the duration of the course students were challenged to explore issues of inequality and devised several strategies to address issues and concerns they saw as pertinent to their communities. We were also challenged to investigate policies and practices that directly affected young people in schools (i.e., the DREAM Act, teacher pay, immigration, homelessness, discipline policies, etc.). Standing in the face of recent CPS data where less than 30 percent of CPS graduating seniors are admitted to four-year colleges and universities, twenty-two of the twenty-six graduating seniors (77 percent) enrolled in the course received admission to four-year institutions.

For many of us who work with communities, families, and young people, we need to recognize the potential disconnects we may have experience with them. Where we can experience deep and tangible connections with young people in the fight for justice in education, there are other spaces where generational divisions are apparent. Instead of viewing this reality as a point of contention, these sites should be viewed as spaces of recognition and accountability. At this moment teachers have the opportunity to create a space where they can learn from their students. In my own classroom, I have numerous technological challenges that my students often correct. Additionally, if I do not understand a term or a position that they are communicating, I ask them to explain or demonstrate how the term is used. This process of "putting me on" was integral to strengthening relationships with my students, allowing me to experience a level of comfort in dealing with my own ignorance in reference to their understandings.

Because discussion was an integral component of the course, many of our conversations would focus on their understandings as young people. Because I'm older, our dialogues and reflections allowed me to realize how much the world has changed for young people. Where many concerns remain the same (i.e., food, clothing, shelter, employment, education, self-determination, peace of mind, etc.), there are nuances that deserve some attention. Technology, through access and distribution, conflates and democratizes many dimensions of the world. In the same light, policies aimed at repressing youth, have also intensified. Instead of looking this as a disconnect, I used it as a space for solidarity. If our concern is liberation, we cannot hold on to the sentiment of "things were better in my day." Instead, we must understand the times as different and should embrace the idea that the new understandings of young people have the potential to serve as sights for liberation. The idea is not to privilege, fetishize, or romanticize the contributions of young people. Instead, the sentiment should be to recognize their contributions. If used properly, our experiences can provide some insight to the questions young people may have concerning their lives. By providing guidance through examples, spaces like a college-bridge class have the potential to contribute to the liberation of our minds for the purposes of engaging the broad project of social justice in education. In the same vein, despite their stated likes of the course, they also offered an important critique. They still felt that my teaching was too lecture-driven and did not incorporate enough hands-on, project-based activities. They felt that I had "deep" knowledge of the subject matter, but sometimes I struggled to communicate my points. In the attempt to reframe relevant, justice-centered teaching, willingness to improve on my shortcomings must be the starting point if I am to have any hope in working toward a justice condition.

More importantly, I have to be critical of my own teaching. No matter how good I may have felt about a particular lesson, my teaching still needs serious work. Throughout the course, there were attendance issues that had to be dealt with. Having a group of seniors during first period presents a set of challenges, especially if the students feel as if they don't have a reason to be there.   Where I it would be irresponsible not to address the issue, it was one that deserved attention, especially in the process of developing structure and a culture of engagement in the course. To simply teach the students that show up while ignoring the others is reminiscent of practices engaged in other schools that only teach the students that come. Once I started to talk to students about why they were coming late, I got the range of answers, revealing that some had to work late shifts while others felt that the course wasn't connected to credits that would count toward graduation. Instead of completely blaming the students, I have to consider my part in the fact that maybe I didn't communicate the college-credit component fully. Because responsibility is shared in the liberatory project of education, blame cannot be placed on students and families absent accountability from teachers and administrators.

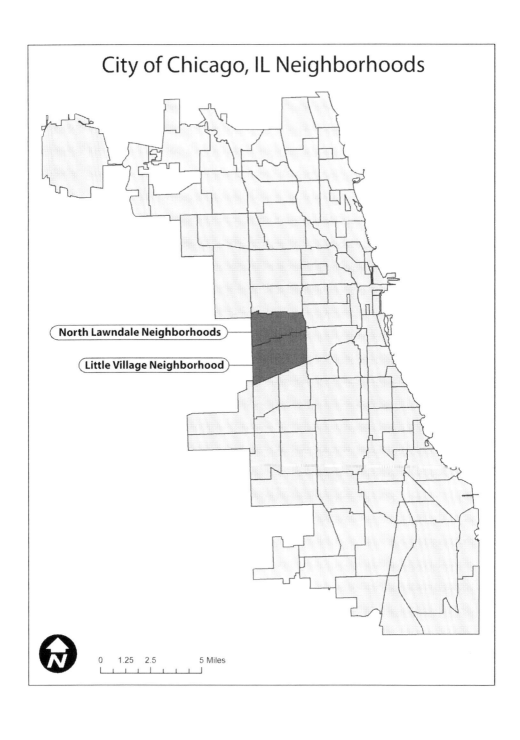

City of Chicago, IL Neighborhoods

North Lawndale Neighborhoods

Little Village Neighborhood

0   1.25   2.5   5 Miles

Chapter 6

Struggle, Failure, and Reflection in the First Cycle (2003–2009)

Practical Lessons in Creating a School

Some days teaching sucks—you totally fail, . . . You may even have a whole semester where the dynamic in the classroom is terrible and you go home everyday embarrassed and ashamed of yourself and your class . . . Every once in a while I would see glimmers of my high school students getting positive feedback and feeling really motivated. But I also saw other people pushing them back down. For so many of my students, their whole lives have been a training in resiliency. I guess the challenge is trying to refocus their and our energy so that school can serve as a place that generates positive experiences for the students and teachers.

—Connie North, *Teaching for Social Justice?*

At the end of my class in the Summer of 2009, I didn't know if I got anywhere close to Yamamoto's notion of a race praxis, where capacity is developed in communities to critically analyze issues of racism/White supremacy while building strategies to address an identified issue. For the majority of the time in ED 196, I often felt that I should be thankful that my students actually put up with me. Recognizing my inadequacies, my course felt more like the process of fumbling ideas and concepts into some coherent semblance of justice-centered curriculum. As a harsh reminder of the realities of teaching, my mistakes heavily outweighed the moments of clarity. When I expressed this to a trusted colleague, she reminded me that now I understood what the first couple of years of teaching are really about. In the attempt to push theory to consider the necessary work on the ground with communities, the idea was to pair CRP with liberatory theories (critical pedagogy, critical youth participatory action research, critical feminist theory, etc.) to create a critical community praxis. Included in this process is the idea that action and reflection in the world in order to change it (praxis) can come by way of engaging community members in a process that places their issues and concerns at the center. Despite the fact that this process is fraught with mistakes and wrong turns, centering the initial mission of the hunger strike was critical to the process of remaining responsible to a community-driven effort.

In doing so, my attempt was to utilize the concept of critical hope offered by Duncan-Andrade (2009) offered in his critique and challenge following the 2008 presidential election of Barack Obama. The idea was to move beyond the idea of "hokey" hope that "ignores the laundry list of inequities that impact the lives of urban youth" (Duncan-Andrade 2009, 2). Because schools in many cases are structurally incapable of addressing the real-life conditions of young people, the attempt to create an institution that operates to the contrary is a serious undertaking. Understanding that the building of a neighborhood high school "cannot, by itself, provide the healing and long-term sustenance required to maintain hope amid conditions of suffering," my classroom contribution was the attempt to interrupt the common master narrative shared concerning students of color in urban space (ibid., 3).

Through the process of engaging students daily with curriculum aimed at questioning status quo, it is not yet known if my students found their experience to be liberating. If hope is medically considered to be a sense of "control of destiny," I am not sure as if my class engendered this with my students (ibid., 4). Instead, I can state that my efforts, no matter how flawed, did receive some approval from the students during the course of the school year. Operating from the premise that hope needs to be supported materially, the course was an attempt to provide young people with resources and skills to address their real-world conditions. If one of the elements of social justice is encapsulated in the ability of young people to make informed decisions for themselves, skill development through critical analysis, reflection, writing, and group project development stood as the "material" resources for students in ED 196. Despite my inhibitions and feelings of inadequacy at times, I also must submit that the "results" of my teaching are not always experienced in the immediate future. For all the times when they are, there are just as many times when they are not.

Again, I am clear that it is not constructive behavior to completely lambaste myself as a horrible teacher. I also agree with Duncan-Andrade that "we must take great risks and accept great challenges if we are going to be effective in urban schools" (ibid., 8). However, at the same time, I know that justice does not occur at the advent of one course. Instead, because the larger project of justice in education is protracted, reflection must be understood as part of the process toward conscientization, or the development of critical consciousness (Freire 1973). Included in the concept of an "audacious" critical hope is the idea of solidarity and "defies the dominant ideology of defense, entitlement, and preservation of privileged bodies at the expense of the policing, disposal, and dispossession of marginalized others" (Duncan-Andrade 2009, 9). If these are the steps toward improvement, developing my critical consciousness should also be considered an act of solidarity with residents of La Villita and North Lawndale. I agree with Duncan-Andrade that

> Audacious hope stares down the painful path; and despite the overwhelming odds against us making it down that path to change, we make the journey again and again. There is no other choice. Acceptance of this fact allows us to find the courage and the commitment to cajole our students to join us on that journey. This makes us better people as it makes us better teachers, and it models for our students that the painful path *is* the hopeful path. (ibid., 13)

Returning to the Solorzano and Yosso tenets in the introduction, my teaching was centered in the attempt to interrupt the commonly shared narrative concerning students of color in urban space. Knowing the project of justice is an unfinished one, my reflections on this time as class instructor are meaningful, but also demands scrutiny.

Process, Implementation, and Navigational Capital

Because my reflections on my course are but a portion of the entirety of the SOJO experience, there are numerous lessons that arose from the formation of the design teams to the first graduating class of 2009. In those lessons are the realities of perpetually navigating the cauldrons of CPS, along with state and federal education policies, all operating under the guise of neoliberalism and White supremacy. As perpetually contested space, there are always issues and concerns that have the potential to close the school or reconfigure it to a place that is the furthest iteration from its original premise. The recurring theme of closure, and its proximity to the faculty and staff of SOJO loomed large in the first four years of the school. Instead of submitting to conspiracy theories abound, we paid close attention to the language and actions of central office, no matter how contradictory. At one point we were awarded special status and at another juncture we were placed on probation. Over time, we felt as if we were subject to the revolving door of central office leadership: one day you're in their good graces, and the next day you're not.

In order to withstand this process, we were very intentional about incorporating what Yosso calls "navigational capital," or the ability to "maneuver through social institutions" (Yosso 2005, 80). From the principal, to teachers, students, families and me, we found ourselves in a perpetual state of navigating CPS, perpetually addressing any requirements brought before us. In our first four years we were constantly bombarded with compliance from the central office. Soon after, we were presented with the challenges of working with students from two adjacent neighborhoods in a hypersegregated city, with few tangible connections to each other. In some of these moments, tensions were high at the school, community, and policy level. By asking tough, pointed questions of my positions as researcher, teacher, and community member, the remaining sections return to the questions posed in the introduction and documents my reflections in relationship to CRT and CRP as pathways to critical community praxis.

Researcher Accountability to Community-Driven Efforts

From the hunger strike forward, I remained leery of the embodiment of an "imposter" status. Because I am neither from La Villita nor North Lawndale, I still served as a member of the design team. In some instances I would render myself voiceless, feeling as if my silence was more important in being respective of community struggle and my perpetually held position as outsider due to my university affiliation. Despite my own misgivings, I was reassured by parents, teachers, and students that my original investment in the struggle demanded that I continue to contribute to the life of the school. In the attempt to document this process, this space had to be continuously renegotiated. Similar to indigenous/First Nations scholar Andrea Smith, I had to realize that "liberation and decolonization are not 'things' that can be taught; they are processes we must practice" (Smith in Sudbury and Ozakawa-Rey 2009, 51). In light of this reality, it became critically important for me to return to the original vision of the hunger strike in creating a school that would intentionally interrupt the aforementioned master narrative.

For these reasons, at every occasion I had to engage in active resistance to research in the traditional sense. I agree that research performed in the positivist tradition "steals knowledge from others and then uses it to benefit the people who stole it" (Tuhiwai Smith 2012, 59). Instead of compiling a book for personal gain in the position of university professor (tenure, book awards, recognition from local and national organizations, etc.), more important is the process of documenting the successes and challenges of a community driven effort supported by university researchers. Instead of research in the positivist tradition to arrogantly assume "ownership of the entire world," my work at SOJO attempts to stand in solidarity with what Tuhiwai Smith refers to as "struggle."

I agree that struggle is a "dynamic, powerful and important tool" (60). At the same time, struggle also calls for recognition of the myriad contradictions that are often present. In my own case, on the surface it may not appear as if I'm struggling. Holding a well-compensated and tenured position at a Research-1 university is definitely not the place to claim struggle to meet basic needs of food, clothing, and shelter. Simultaneously, it is also dangerous and incorrect to claim the academy as a place of solitude that miraculously releases one from the grip of White supremacy/racism. Although people can become blinded by the nominal "perks" of faculty employment, postraciality is neither real nor utilitarian in community-centered work. Because we are racialized in almost every aspect of our lives, there is unequivocally no sound reason to think that the academy offers anything to the contrary. Because it does not, it becomes even more important to name the spaces and events that speak to the legacy of overt and covert exclusion of communities of color from creating collective spaces to heal and build. In terms of research, Tang (2009) is correct that it has the potential to become powerful if it is "connected to a radical examination of academic privilege and standards" (Tang in Cole 2009, 257). However, commitment in this sense requires recognition of the problematic nature of positivism in academia if left unchallenged.

Understanding where I rest on the continuum of struggle is important in navigating the tensions/contradictions of university and community. In relation to my involvement at SOJO, I resonate with Tuhiwai Smith's comments that

> In its broader sense struggle is simply what life feels like when people are trying to survive in the margins, to seek freedom

> from better conditions, to seek social justice. Struggle is a tool
> of both social activism and theory. It is a tool that has the
> potential to enable oppressed groups to embrace and mobilize
> agency, and to turn the consciousness of injustice into strategies
> for change . . . It can provide the mean for working things out
> 'on the ground,' for identifying and solving problems of practice,
> for identifying strengths and weaknesses, for refining tactics and
> uncovering deeper challenges. (Tuhiwai Smith 2012, 199)

Knowing that the *huelgistas* were involved in a struggle to seek better educational conditions for young people in their community, another question
arises in terms of the work needed to support such struggle beyond the
initial hunger strike. CRT and CRP were critical elements to my process,
in that they allowed for a space to engage the contradictions of academic research and grapple with the realities of White supremacy/racism in
education. Beyond the rhetorical gaze, the challenge was to centralize the
understanding that "people, families, (and) organizations in marginalized
communities struggle everyday" (200). Research, as the site where agency,
structure, ethics, and method intersect, provides an interesting place for
knowledge to be produced and engaged. From my first participation on
the design team to the first graduating class, research in support of justice
remained "an intellectual, cognitive, and moral project, often fraught, never
complete but worthwhile" (215).

Justice in Contested Space

Because school development in big city school systems is perpetually contested space, I am reminded of the necessity of accountability. Making sure
that my own political clarity allows me to develop and align tangible work
to community-driven struggles, I must contend with the various tensions in
the process. As researcher and concerned community member, such clarity
comes in the form of resisting the paradigm of researching with "subjects"
and on a "research site." Where some are satisfied with this as meeting
the traditional rules of research, the radical project of engaged research
wrestles with real-life contradictions that have the opportunity to deeply
impact the educational well-being of a school. Explained in detail in the
introduction, chapter 4 and continued in the next chapter, we (SOJO faculty, administration, staff, families, and students) constantly wrestled with
the tensions of enacting a justice-centered project in CPS. As the central

office actively takes every opportunity to remind us of the fact that the four newly created schools should only be understood as CPS schools, we perpetually exist under the auspices of the state. Throughout the process and in the current moment, the contestation comes in the form of new achievement requirements, new curricular approvals at the state and federal level, and the political will to dissolve schools in the same vein as SOJO. In our first year there was the ACT college readiness standards. Soon after two tests were added to the battery of standardized tests for students (the EXPLORE assessment for incoming freshman and PLAN for sophomores). These were both assessments added with the required ACT requirement for all CPS students. Additionally, CPS created three sets of different rubrics to go with two sets of central office administrations in our first four years of operation (Arne Duncan and Ron Huberman). Because most of these neoliberal "innovations" and assessment tools contribute little or nothing to the educative process, we are still required to navigate these policies and requirements in perpetuity.

This makes for trying times for students, faculty and families. Observing this from the positions of researcher, coteacher, ALSC member, and collaborator, in some instances this made for an uneasy environment as tensions rose and fell with every new requirement from central office. Operating in a situation with many moving parts, the rumor mill of the central office would often keep us guessing what the next move would be in terms of whether or not the school would remain a small school or be consolidated into a comprehensive high school. Changing the frame from participant observer to observant participant, I leaned on Vargas's notion of the observant participant to be one that my observation of SOJO became one of the "appendage(s) of the main activity" of making sure the school continued to serve the students and families of La Villita and North Lawndale (Vargas in Cole 2008, 175).

Our constantly rumored consolidation often hinged on CPS's rationale that the four schools in the multiplex were too expensive to maintain. Coupled with the fact that our CHRSI funds ran out by the beginning of 2008, there were numerous concerns about our ability to continue programming in the way we initially envisioned in the proposal to CPS. These were funds used for retreat programming, supplies, and overtime pay. Once these funds expired, the things we used to enhance our programming were now unavailable. No longer did we have funds to take staff on retreats for professional development where they could collectively plan curriculum. Additionally, funds used for any additional resources in the forms of supplemental curriculum texts and technology were no longer available. Like many material possessions, once we became accustomed to the "perks" afforded by the supplemental funding, to work without them required everyone to make adjustments. Collective planning became more difficult as teachers were spread thin from not having the time allotted in the professional development retreats. Where supplemental curricular texts allowed for teachers to use materials beyond the allotted budgetary line item, staff had to become more resourceful in locating texts that were once available for direct purchase. To some, this is all too common in the day-to-day struggles of a neighborhood high school. As faculty and staff made the necessary adjustments, some were more difficult to do without the supplemental funding. Collective planning time across departments is of particular importance as it provides the ability to supply students with interdisciplinary content. This was also one of the original visions articulated in the proposal submitted to CPS. To the staff's credit, despite the challenges set forth by our loss of funds, many were forward thinking in their approach to our diminishing finances. At one point, the administration and staff created an external non-profit to independently raise funds for the school. Adding further irony, the Gates Foundation, after investing millions in CPS, has since pulled out of funding public neighborhood schools altogether. Currently they have shifted their efforts to the neoliberal strategies of school turnaround, merit-based teacher pay, teacher quality, and school choice (Lipman 2011, 101).

More than the monetary resources themselves, it is important to understand the process as layered and multifaceted. Instead of unilateral, causal relationships, school creation and implementation function as a set of multifaceted encounters that require serious attention at numerous levels. As a school for social justice operating in a system that has historically engaged in injustice by way of disinvestment and destabilization, we are often challenged to sit with the contradictions. Because we exist in a system (CPS) that does not extoll social justice as one of its primary tenets, we were constantly asked by the central office, "what is a school of social justice anyway?" Furthermore, central office only expects compliance with the new requirements of the state. Any pushback from local schools places a figurative bull's-eye on its back for the remainder of its days. When we pushed back on our inclusion in Renaissance 2010, CPS's professional development and curricular frameworks, we knew that it would not be without consequence. Existing as a CPS school, many of the faculty agreed that we would perpetually have to fight the idea of becoming "regular school." Among faculty, becoming "regular school" meant that SOJO was under threat of transitioning into an institution that centered itself solely in the basic "order and compliance" required from the district to keep the doors open. Separate from the individual efforts of teachers in their respective classrooms, standing as a collective school to defend justice-centered education required consistent check-ins and updates that kept faculty abreast of any new movements from the central office or Chicago's political machine. If there was no concerted effort to do so, dissention would soon follow, making it easier to undermine the initial effort to create the multiplex.

These challenges, while real, are indicative of any attempt to maintain the intentionality of community-driven struggle. Amid the numerous layers, the battle is always against co-optation. Because we are a CPS school, there were moments where we felt as if we were slowly becoming "regular school." State requirements in the form of testing, discipline, standards, and the necessary compliance forms for federal funding (Title I and Title VI) are concretized requirements. In our case (as is the case of many others), maintaining responsibility to the original hunger strike requires thoughtful navigation rooted in transparency. Where this is the goal, it is not always reality. Neoliberal corporate education reform requires the co-optation language and bodies to enact market-driven solutions to the issue at hand. I concur with Anyon (2005) that given the "recent global, neoliberal mandates to privatize social services like education . . . the systemic problems of urban education require more attention to pedagogy, curriculum and assessment" (Anyon 2005, 61). At first the neoliberal hegemons (coupled with the state) have attempted to hide in "plain sight." Now they are emboldened to take control of the discourse regarding educational innovations that have had success at the community level. Child/parent centers, restorative justice, small schools, teacher-driven professional development, and student-centered learning have been replaced by "digital instructional solutions," "personalized learning," "competition," and "global talent assessment" (www.pearson.com/about-us/education/north-america.html). These current trends continue to serve as reminders that active resistance to these developments is challenging and does not guarantee positive results.

Theory to Action While Falling

The imagery of "falling" is central to my understanding because the blows endured from the central office could give you the feeling that you were repeatedly taking blows to the face in a boxing match. CPS, while slow to deliver accolades on justice-centered education, was quick to remind us of how we were out of compliance with whatever machination they put forward. In some cases, this resulted in the threat of academic probation and the threat of removal of key resources. For these reasons, I had to be very intentional in finding support for my efforts throughout the process. Whereas I saw my work in the struggle to create SOJO as largely supporting students, family, and staff at SOJO through the acquisition and utilization of resources, the community of researchers doing similar work were key to my personal sustenance in my efforts throughout the initiative.

In the explicit attempt to transition CRP from legal scholarship to educational inquiry at the community level, Yamamoto's use of critical pragmatism is of maximum importance to my work at SOJO. Borrowing from Mari Matsuda, this pragmatism

> Emphasizes multiple consciousness, experience, flexibility, and context; that engages the experiences and stories of those habitually on society's margins, not because those experiences and stories are more worthy but because in mainstream justice discourse they tend to be minimized. (Matsuda in Yamamoto 1999, 135)

By replacing "justice" with "education" in the aforementioned epigraph, the parallels are evident in the current moment of standards and neoliberal reform. My process coincides with Yamamoto in that "traditional theories of justice tend to be highly abstract and speak past day-to-day social realities" (Yamamoto, 142). They also "tend to translate poorly into concrete approaches to understanding and addressing real-life racial conflicts and prospects of remediation or healing" (ibid.). This being the case, I found myself in constant consultation with others who've made a conscious commitment to foreground community need over adulation from the research community. They're understanding of the current moment in education coupled with concrete classroom and administrative practice, provided the necessary foundation by which to engage our work at SOJO. In terms of my own positioning, the ability to physically engage and observe the work of these communities in person provided me the necessary examples that would allow me to engage in the role of researcher and observant participant. Because many of these spaces was supported by university researchers in the initial stages (e.g., East Oakland Community High School, Raza Studies in Tucson, etc.) the ability to discuss their triumphs and mistakes was invaluable. In the instances of Oakland and Tucson, where the respective institutions and programs were fighting for their collective lives, observation of the opposition to their efforts were invaluable. From their process I learned that it is never an issue of "if" the powers that be will challenge your existence. Instead, it is always an issue of "when" our position of justice-centered education would be challenged by the central office.

Trudging Forward

I offer my reflections on the process as recognition of the multilayered relationships between university, community, students, families, staff, and administration. Throughout this process, we realized that beyond the edifice of the multiplex building that houses SOJO and the other three schools, it is also a space comprised and ran by humans, rendering it a living and breathing thing.

At the same time, and indicative to most grassroots community efforts for justice-centered education, the human element of our work brings inter-relational struggles and challenges. This results in spaces where people dis-agree and sometimes feel as if they are pushed to their wit's end. Where this was not a persistent occurrence throughout the process, there were situations that resulted in people leaving the school altogether, never to return. As in most organizing work, tensions arise when the initial goal is achieved (in our case the building of the school), and the subsequent work required to maintain the spirit of the original initiative as the work moves forward. Luckily for us, through the TAC process, there were *huelgistas* and community members on the TAC to maintain continuity to the commu-nity-driven initiative. Because the hunger strike could not be a permanent event, encapsulating the spirit responsible for its genesis had its share of challenges. As the TAC transitioned and approved the design teams, there was concern that the initial intent of the hunger strike would be lost as the process was placed in the responsibility of CPS. At SOJO, there was an intentional effort in the first four years of existence (and beyond) to make sure the hunger strike was a central element in the operations of the school. From the murals and mosaics in the SOJO corridor, to the English and social studies curriculum, which required all freshmen to interact with the hunger strikers for the creation of a course assignment, to the Essential 7 awards, to our first graduation, staff and administration were intentional in their inclusion of their knowledge of the efforts that brought the school into fruition. As *huelgistas* were also members of the ALSC, their insights were critical, as many were very familiar with the functions of CPS from the community and parent level. Discussed in detail in the next chapter, this also resulted in tensions with other ALSC members, as the school met with challenges from the central office. These tensions were deeply seated in race, class, and position.

Returning to Yamamoto's race praxis, I cannot be dismissive of the tensions as just those that are germane to the process of maintaining responsibility to community-driven efforts. Instead, each set of tensions have their own set of nuances that bring about a different set of reactions to the conflict. Because SOJO houses African-American and Latino/a students in a school located in a predominantly Latino/a neighborhood, these tensions and the pain brought forward from the process deserve particular attention. Because this pain brings about feelings of anger and hurt, healing becomes important. As a collective we weren't always the best with our intentionality with healing, but there was an attempt to provide an understanding between groups experiencing the conflict. Utilizing Yamamoto's four dimensions of racial justice (recognition, responsibility, reconstruction, and reparation), the first three deeply resonate with struggle, healing, and the process to bring SOJO to fruition.

The first dimension of recognition "asks racial groups members to recognize, and empathize with, the anger and hope of those wounded" (Yamamoto 1999, 174). This was critical in the first years of the school as African-American residents from North Lawndale were brought into the process under the constraints of CPS's interpretation of a federal consent decree. This brought about issues of distrust as members from both communities were unfamiliar with each other. For North Lawndale residents, the process felt rushed, as community members were only provided with a nominal knowledge of the efforts in La Villita. Authentic community engagement was difficult to obtain under the auspices of creating attendance boundaries, ensuring a student population that was at least 30 percent African-American. The inclusion of members from North Lawndale ebbed and flowed throughout, but this recognition is important to the overall process.

The second dimension of responsibility "asks racial groups to assess carefully the dynamics of racial group agency imposing disabling constraints on others, and, when appropriate, accepting group responsibility for healing wounds" (ibid.). This became critically important when tensions between students escalated into physical fights. In Chicago, hypersegregation also brings about neighborhood and street organization (gang) tensions. In order to be intentional in addressing these conflicts, as faculty and administration we had to engage in difficult conversations on race. An initial mistake occurred when we tried to address it with students first, before confronting it as staff and administration. Learning the lesson from our first mistake, we developed a process by which to proactively address racial tensions at the faculty and student level. Addressing these concerns brought us into the third dimension of reconstruction, which includes "active steps toward healing the social and psychological wounds resulting from disabling group constraints" (175). In this process we were responsible for "remaking and retelling stories about self, the other and interactions" (198). Again, operating under the White supremacist/racist structure of society, our counterstories were realized in our attempt to reimagine and implement the possibilities of what community centered, justice-driven education could be.

What of the "Real Life" Conditions Faced by Communities in Troubling Times?

In the introduction, I posed the question about the ways in which CRT/CRP can make tangible connections to people's lives. As theory, it allows for us to engage the ways in which racism/White supremacy operates as an ideological construct while coupled with other forms of oppression (in this particular case, class, and gender). Where CPS is comprised of people, the superstructure of the city of Chicago and public education has operated to perpetually limit access and opportunity for low-income Black and Latino/a residents. Regarding praxis, CRT/CRP in education allows for those who engage the construct to grapple with the ways in which the work on the ground connects to the real-life conditions of those who are experiencing suffering at the hands of the state.

The process of community engagement can be uneven, complicated, and trying. However, the tangible results are realized in the lasting relationships developed with communities in addressing their needs—hence forging the commitment to social justice. If my own attempts do not honor and articulate the messy imperfections of community engaged research, I do disservice to those currently doing the work and those who seek to engage in similar work in the future. For it is from these spaces that we get the lessons so drastically needed to improve our collective condition. Discussed in detail in the next chapter, such commitments beg difficult questions about our spiritual, mental, and physical selves.

Chapter 7

Always on the Run

School Struggle in Perpetuity

In light of my reflections in chapter 6 on the years from the design team to SOJO's first graduating class, the following chapter presents a set of counterstories to highlight the continual intricacies of SOJO in relation to the neoliberal rationales of a large school district in the age of austerity in Chicago. The complex, moving pieces that comprise the CPS central administration creates an instance where SOJO is continually at the whim of neoliberal sentiment and White supremacy, largely through standards-based school reform and budget cuts. Through a very engrained technology of racism as state policy, the most radical of educational projects are soon framed as failures, while corporate "reformers" are not only given the opportunity to fail, but fail on numerous occasions if their political alignments are in concert with the mayor's office. Returning to the discussion of political economy in the introduction, Educational Management Organization conglomerates (EMOs) are able to secure contracts with the city, guaranteeing narrow, "data-driven" academic achievement in the form of standardized test scores and rigid alignment with state standards. In Chicago, these arrangements are most notably located in EMOs like the Noble Charter Network, United Neighborhood Organization (UNO—a former community organizing collective), and the Academy of Urban School Leadership (AUSL). Their network of schools are positioned as the "viable" alternative to neighborhood public schools, as they offer rigid compliance and success via college admissions or substantial increases in test score performance.

Simultaneously, UNO, led by Juan Rangel, had repeatedly expressed its interest in having a school in the building. Under the banner of UNO, Rangel secured $100 million from the State of Illinois to proliferate their brand of charters throughout Chicago (cite and note). Rangel's brand of

charter school centers its rationale of achievement through the "Americaniza-
tion" of Latino/a families, playing on the stereotype of the "hard working,
deserving" families that take advantage of opportunities, unlike their Black
counterparts to the North (in Rangel's rationale). Using our navigational
skills, we alerted elected officials that the current manifestations at SOJO
primed us for closure and for the potential of UNO stepping in. Understanding how opposed the alderman was to charter schools and his history
with UNO, we figured this to be a point to accentuate in our struggles.
Knowing that he understood families in both neighborhoods of North
Lawndale and La Villita to stand in opposition to charters, we felt there
was a chance to strengthen our alliance with him as the resistance developed.

Where my example is specific to Chicago, neoliberalism in this case
comes in the form of corporate school reform, which has implications for
cities across the country. As Chicago is looked as the "model" for combin-
ing the housing and education "markets" as stages for urban development,
education plays a pivotal role as cities look to solidify and bifurcate service-
sector employment among its most affluent and marginalized residents (i.e.,
Philadelphia, New Orleans, Pittsburgh, New York, Los Angeles, Detroit,
Newark, etc.). Incorporating the language of failure, public education has
been deemed a "failed experiment" desperately in need of "innovation."
Despite minimal success, these "innovations" have resulted in further marginalization of communities that have historically had the least access to
resources and state infrastructure.

Framed explicitly in the work of the Collaborative for Equity and Justice (CEJE) and the Kenwood Oakland Community Organization (KOCO),
the following three counterstories are couched in their "three Ds" of corporate school reform: disenfranchisement, disinvestment, and destabilization
(Lipman & KOCO, 2012). Intimately connected to the three Ds occurring
throughout the city in other schools serving low-income/working-class communities of color, SOJO's story is unfortunately one of many in a hypersegregated, politically charged city. Fortunately, the community of students,
parents, and staff took matters into their own hands. All of the involved were
prepared for an elongated battle with CPS to make sure the original mission
and vision of the school was protected and did not succumb to the current
downsizing trend in the district. In order to do so, there needed to be a
concerted effort to organize, making sure our planning remained strategic
to the concerns of the school and the building. Similar to Yamamoto's call
for Critical Race Praxis (CRP) I found myself at the moment where theory
was put to work to guide my practice in working with students, families,
teachers, and community members.

Relevant to the larger political economy of the city, the events at SOJO from the spring semester of 2010 to the summer of 2013 are of particular significance. Because SOJO is a neighborhood public school that serves fewer than four hundred students, the city's claim of budget shortfalls ranging between $700 and $800 million often deems the school "too expensive" to operate (personal communication). Despite the fact that public dollars are ciphered away from CPS's budget to fund the new bevy of charter and contract schools, neighborhood public schools often bear the brunt of the supposed budget shortfall. Coupled with the fact that SOJO shares the building with three other schools, CPS has continually argued that a more cost-effective arrangement would be a consolidation of the four schools into one comprehensive high school. Having four separate principals and staff is deemed too expensive for a group of students that collectively, as all four schools, would compose a medium-sized comprehensive high school in Chicago (between 1,400 and 1,600 students). Contributing to the rationale for consolidation is fluctuating test score performance that in some cases may not meet CPS's requirements for annual yearly progress. In Chicago, if a school has a history of declining test scores, it is placed on probation. If a school is on probation for more than three years, the Board of Education (under the guise of CPS's CEO with final approval from the mayor's office) could choose to close the school or subject it to "turnaround," where all the staff is fired and invited to reapply (Morales-Doyle, 2013). Discussed in detail in later sections, the rhetoric of underutilization has further complicated matters, as the district has moved to close forty-nine schools in the Spring of 2013.

Disinvestment: If There's a Hell Below— Budget Shortfalls and Purposeful Neglect

Following a school year of relative calm (2009–2010), SOJO's principal was alerted to looming budget cuts from the central office. As students and teachers wound down from the 2009–2010 school year, we received the news that we would have to eliminate five teacher positions, including our assistant principal (Cynthia Nambo, original coordinator of the design teams), our literacy coach, and one of our college counselors. Whereas this would be a tremendous loss at a comprehensive high school, the results of the budget shortfall are intensified as any disruption of an already small faculty can make for particular difficulties regarding instructional support and school culture.

Due to the strength of the community-driven effort, SOJO still makes a concerted effort to operate according to the community's original vision for the school. However, in SOJO's fourth year, the removal of the school's first principal (Rito Martinez) serves as the catalyst for the cycle of the three Ds. Of particular importance to this section is disinvestment, as the resources removed from the school begins a process that speaks to the removal of resources from SOJO in the name of austerity budgets and other costly district expenditures.

Furthering disinvestment was the ending of SOJO's Autonomous Management Program School (AMPS) status. As an AMPS school, CPS provides flexibility in curriculum planning, resource alignment, along with offering a stipend for schools selected to participate in the program. As a small school, autonomy and funding (chapter 2) from CHSRI would allow the principal and staff to maintain programming (e.g., colloquium from chapter 4), and utilize funds for student and family needs (e.g., Federal Financial Aid workshops for families, monetary support for student-family nights adult education courses, etc.).

The subsequent layoffs necessitated by disinvestment led to a sense of distrust between the staff and the school's second principal. Due to increased pressure from CPS to comply with city and state standards (ACT College Readiness Standards, increased reliance on standardized test score performance as the primary determinant of academic achievement, etc.), the faculty felt as if factions had begun to develop. Some sided with the principal's new push to meet CPS and state accountability, while others felt as if the new trend would further push the school away from its original mission and vision. These real and perceived factions deepened tensions between Blacks and Latino/as, while simultaneously threatening the collaborative environment central to the foundation of the school.

Furthering the destabilization, SOJO experienced an unprecedented turnover/loss of one third of the staff in the spring of 2010. Continuing the strategy of disinvestment, three key positions were never restored. The loss of Cynthia Nambo as assistant principal (responsible for design and implementation of curricular alignment), in addition to an effective English teacher, a split math/science position and a vacated literacy coach position that went unfilled (CPS eliminated the position districtwide) led directly to a flattening of academic achievement. Coupled with a drop in attendance, SOJO was placed on probation in the fall of 2011. The pressure of being on probation, declining staff morale, and the loss of AMPS status and CHSRI funding proved too heavy for the second principal, who made the decision to resign at the end of the first quarter in 2011 (Morales-Doyle, 2012).

Disenfranchisement: Collective Responses
to Burnout, Departure, and Flux

October 21, 2011, Minneapolis, Minnesota: While having dinner the night before a workshop presentation for Minneapolis public school teachers, I noticed a text message from a SOJO teacher. It read, "the principal came in and announced his resignation today." My first response was to curse and yell out loud, but I looked across the table to my partner and told her the news. As her eyes widened with shock, I excused myself to call the teacher. During our conversation he explained to me that the principal called an emergency faculty meeting and explained to everyone that he had enough of his position as principal and was calling it quits. Granted, I knew that there had been tensions among the staff regarding our new attention to test scores and college readiness standards, and that the principal was not pleased with his relationship with the staff, many of whom he became close with before his transition to principal (he moved up the ranks at SOJO from teacher to assistant principal to principal).

This put the school in a serious predicament; not only were we on academic probation, we would have to engage a principal search in the first quarter of the school year. It is especially difficult to do this when most viable candidates traditionally make themselves eligible for hiring in the summer. Complicating this is the fact that CPS's Office of Principal Professional Development (OPPD) developed a new battery of qualifications for principal candidates. If an applicant does not pass the initial set of requirements (which includes a series of observations and tests), the person cannot become "principal eligible." For the ALSC, this became a problem because we could only choose potential candidates to interview who were currently on the principal eligibility list. Coupled with the idea that we were already "too expensive" by CPS standards (four schools with four administrations were positioned as a strain on CPS's budget), we entertained a worst-case scenario. Our inability to find a viable principal could leave us with a series of interim administrators who would not understand the mission and vision of the school, potentially derailing what was built over the last seven years and making the environment hostile and toxic. Additionally, fearing the current trend of closures in CPS under the guise of Renaissance 2010, the lethal combination of being too expensive, on academic probation, and without a principal would make SOJO a prime candidate for closure. At the time of the principal's announcement of his resignation, over seventy schools had been closed or declared "turnaround," in which the entire faculty is removed and replaced by a new administration and faculty. Ironically, this development has not resulted in any sort of improvement in school achievement (Lipman 2011).

Upon returning to Chicago, we convened as the ALSC understanding the particular restraints placed on us in light of new CPS policies. We dedicated ourselves to learning as much as we could about the principal hiring process while following leads with people we knew across the city who might consider taking the position. Simultaneously, the outgoing principal, in the attempt to create a situation where there would be the least amount of time between his departure and the hiring of a new administrator, unintentionally created a timeline with a turnaround date that was untenable. Once we got the timeline pushed back, we were able to maneuver to buy ourselves more time. We were offered a stopgap solution in the interim, where the school would have what CPS refers to as an "administrator-in-charge" (AIC)—essentially a retired school principal who has enough workdays left not to jeopardize his or her pension to keep the school running while a new principal is hired. As a blessing in disguise, the AIC was an extremely competent and transparent person. Students and staff were impressed with her ability to address school issues in a fair, but critical manner. Demonstrative of her commitment was her promise to assist the new principal in becoming acclimated to the school.

As the AIC came closer to making her transition, our search process under the aforementioned constraints yielded an extremely small candidate pool. However, because four members of the ALSC were also hunger strikers, they used their deep community networks and found a potential candidate, Ms. Valentino (a pseudonym). Members of the ALSC met with her informally on separate occasions to get an idea of what she brought to the table. She was Latina, from La Villita, bilingual, and had some success in math and science education at the K–8 level. One of the ALSC members went to high school with her and had good things to say about her. Our concern was that in our initial conversations with her, she didn't seem as clear as to how she would tangibly implement SOJO's mission and vision. Most of her responses to our inquiries on social justice involved getting students to graduate and "reaching" the gangbangers who were written off by CPS. Where these could be included in the larger social justice project in education, her inability to articulate a clear vision of how she understood social justice as a concept to be implemented in relation to the mission and vision of the school drew concerns. Nevertheless, we encouraged her to apply for the position.

As more applications came in, we noticed another person who sparked our interest. She had high school experience as a principal and was known for her ability to challenge central office. Ms. Jackson's (a pseudonym) situation was that her school was closed without warning. Due to this experience, she worked with a collective of parents, teachers, students, community organizers, and administrators to the state capital to change legislation on an earlier set of school closings. Because of her collaborative efforts with parents, students, and state legislators, CPS schools cannot be closed without proper warning. This resonated with the ALSC because it appeared as if she had a sense of justice in her understanding of schools. I promised the ALSC that I would try to find out as much as I could about her, but my efforts were unsuccessful.

Both candidates were called in for a first round of interviews. As the ALSC, we knew we needed someone with experience who was willing to resist draconian CPS policies coupled with the skills and ability to execute a strategy to remove us from the list of schools on probation. Though we agreed on these points, there was division on the ALSC as to who could best fulfill these needs. At this moment, SOJO's student body was close to 85 percent Latino/a and 15 percent African-American. Of the ten members of the ALSC at the time, seven were Latino/a, one was mixed-race, and two were African-American. Where there hadn't been any pronounced race or class divisions on the ALSC, the school struggles to attract and retain African-American students, due to the explosion of charter schools in North Lawndale. At the same time, some Latino/a members of the ALSC hold steadfast to the fact that the school is for all students, no matter the race or neighborhood of origin. Like many issues of race and class, there is a subtle underpinning that becomes central to this discussion. Because SOJO is located in La Villita, some community members still envision it as a community school whose priority is the students in that neighborhood specifically. Though these discussions have not been explicit on the ALSC, there have been moments where members have expressed the importance of responsibility to the community of La Villita when making any decisions concerning the school. Contributing further to the tensions on the ALSC is the fact that half of the ALSC has advanced U.S.-based education, creating a strain when discussing the political economy of the city and the potential for SOJO to close. Coupled with a language barrier (Spanish is the primary language of three ALSC members), communication can be strained despite translation provided at ALSC meetings. In the instance of selecting a principal under specific CPS restraints, said tensions are heightened with the pressure of CPS policies and the threat of closure. Whereas the views of some of the ALSC members may be viewed as protectionist, it is understood that many Latinos/as remain marginalized and isolated in CPS and in throughout the city of Chicago. At the same time, a vision of solidarity with African-American residents promotes the rare opportunity to intentionally confront White supremacy through collective visioning and planning in a school. Nevertheless, the tensions that arise, however subtle in the beginning, intensified as members of the ALSC disagreed as to who made the most viable candidate, considering our concerns regarding whether or not CPS would move to close SOJO.

Many of these concerns and sentiment arose in the differing opinions among ALSC members as to what we thought was best for students. Many of the LSC members (including three of the hunger strikers) were concerned about the school's current probation status. Where they liked the outgoing principal as a person, they expressed their disdain for probation. Because the community has witnessed a legacy of underresourced, disinvested schools, SOJO is viewed as a space that should provide the opportunity to reverse the trend. Complicating matters further was the fact that this would be the third principal in three years (including the administrator in charge). After promises made by the outgoing principal to remain at the school, many members of the faculty and the ALSC felt burned by his sudden departure. Ms. Valentino, as someone from the neighborhood who knew the struggles of the community intimately, presented an opportunity to return to keeping the issues and concerns of the community at the center.

In our discussions as the ALSC, I agreed with a number of members that an experienced principal who had a plan to get us off probation would be critical in keeping the school open. Due to the rash of current school closings in Chicago, we knew that many EMOs (namely UNO) would jump at the opportunity to be in the building. SOJO's closing would provide the perfect opportunity to touch down in the building as a "viable educational option" for the community. Additionally, if SOJO were to fail, its closure would represent the fraught nature of community driven efforts, highlighted in their inability to meet state guidelines in instruction. CPS, in its initial paternalistic view of working-class/low-income communities of color, has a broad distrust of community-driven efforts. In their eyes, the closing of SOJO would be yet another testament to the inability of ground-up efforts to understand the complexities of maintaining a school. Despite many examples to the contrary, this paternalistic view is characteristic of White supremacy, which includes creating arbitrary norms as a means to limit the ability of community members to challenge the existing system. For these reasons, as an ALSC we knew that our ability to navigate CPS policy and the contrasting mission and vision of SOJO would be critical in our juncture of securing a new principal. Where there seemed to be a general agreement by members of the ALSC on these concerns, some also expressed the need for a person who had community concerns at the center of their analysis. Because both sides are correct in the analysis, we decided to see how the candidates would fare during the interview process. The hope was that we could get someone who could navigate this delicate, but necessary tension in our situation.

After our first round of interviews, the two finalists that were brought in for full-day interviews and a community forum were Ms. Valentino and Ms. Jackson. During this process each candidate met with students, faculty, community members, and community partners. The community forum at the end of the day was particularly for parents who would not be able to make the meetings at the end of the school day. After fielding feedback via survey and various one-on-one interactions, everyone seemed to be luke-warm about both candidates. At the same time, we were alerted that there were major problems at Ms. Valentino's current school with faculty and community members. Coupled with the fact that she didn't have a grasp of what social justice meant to her, nor a concrete plan on how to recruit and retain African-American students (a lingering problem) and the lack of the ability to address the academic probation situation, this drew a red flag from some of the ALSC members, students, faculty, and community partners.

The concerns with Ms. Jackson were rooted in her expressed belief that one of the pathways to justice included the ability to mobilize local and state legislators to defend public education. Paired with the fact that she was monolingual and did not expand on social justice beyond the ability to mobilize local and state politicians, her strengths and challenges were clear. One strength, however, was her well-articulated plan of recruiting African-American students and concrete short-term and longitudinal strategies on how to address probation. The ALSC felt this was important as we moved forward in finding a long-term principal.

All of these concerns clashed in our ALSC meetings. Because we had the responsibility of submitting a single candidate to CPS, there was a struggle as to whose name would be the final submission. To the Valentino supporters, I reiterated that she didn't have a concrete plan and we were in desperate need of a strategy if SOJO was to keep its doors open. Whereas Jackson was not the ideal candidate for some, her strengths were evident in her plan. Many returned to the fact that it would be difficult for her to understand the concerns of Spanish-speaking parents as a monolingual English speaker. This was a central community concern as schools that serve Latino/a students with Spanish-speaking parents have experienced rampant paternalistic leadership that has not addressed their concerns of transparency with school policy. To Ms. Jackson's credit, she was the principal of a school that was 50 percent Latino/a and 50 percent African-American. During her tenure she kept a robust student population while the three other schools in the building had dwindling student bodies. One of her letters of recommendation was from a Latino/a parent who expressed his satisfaction with her ability to address the concerns of the community despite her inability to speak Spanish.

The final development in the principal hiring culminated in an open meeting with a closed session vote by the ALSC. In attendance were members of community partner organizations, parents, and a central office representative, specifically from the office that supervised LSCs and ALSCs. He informed us that all we needed was a simple majority vote. Because the student ALSC member cannot vote, there were nine eligible voters. As the community representatives expressed their concerns about and their support for both candidates, the meeting was closed for the vote. Each member voted with a show of hands. With nine members present, the vote was 5–4 for Jackson. To the credit of everyone on the ALSC, there was no dispute over the vote. However, the lines were drawn in the sand; the person felt by some to have the community's concerns at heart was not selected.

This left a rift in the ALSC. Some felt that a faction of the group wrongly conspired outside of ALSC meetings to strategize on how to get Jackson elected. Those who voted for Jackson were also accused of making Valentino supporters the enemy by bringing in reinforcements by way of community partners and the central office staff. Where this was furthest from the truth, the perception became the reality in terms of ALSC relations. This was expressed to the new principal in her second ALSC meeting. Where Ms. Jackson respectfully replied that she didn't need to know all of the particulars, Valentino supporters expressed that there was no personal feelings of ill will toward her. They believed in her ability to do her job as SOJO principal, but they would not apply for membership to the ALSC next year. Again, we revisited earlier tensions experienced in the first years of SOJO's existence, where some parents and community members from La Villita remained welcoming of African-American residents from North Lawndale, while others remained "on the fence." This repeating tension, while between Latinos/as and African-Americans, continues to stand as the residuals of a decade-long struggle for community control that has been constrained by White supremacy. Much like the colonial practice of "divide and conquer," the powers that be are able to provide particular political and monetary concessions to Black and Brown communities, simultaneously creating the idea that both groups have special entrée to the mayor's office. In a politically charged city like Chicago, this serves the ideological process of White supremacy as Black and Brown residents are under the belief that each other are in a manufactured epic battle for "limited" resources.

In the end, all of this left a bitter taste in the mouths of those who participated in the principal election. Our decisions, not solely guided by race and ethnicity, ended up being heavily seasoned by them when all was said and done. At the same time, the schools doors are open, but it is never a foregone conclusion as to how long that will be. Despite the constant struggle to remain open, this instance may result in the loss of community input from an active group of the *huelgistas*, who were instrumental to the school's creation.

Destabilization: School Upheaval, Resistance, and a City in Flux

August 7, 2012: In the early afternoon I received a voicemail from Katie Hogan, asking me to give her a call back as soon as I could. As soon as I called her back she alerted me that our newly hired principal was fired. Following my gasping and yelling, she continued to explain that two security guards came into the building, went to the principal's office, handed her a document, and explained that she had forty-five minutes to pack her things and leave. The document handed to the principal was four sentences long, explaining to her that she was an at-will employee and that her services were no longer needed as principal.

Along with Katie, the staff and teachers were gracious enough to place me on speakerphone to be a part of the conversation on what the next steps should be. In these situations, it takes time to get used to the initial shock of the situation, but as our tempers diffused we discussed how we should consider this as part of the plan to consolidate the four schools. This being the case, we felt the next steps would be to demand a meeting with the Alderman Munoz around bringing the principal back to the school, as she was summarily fired with the no known reason. This became the "Rewind to August 9" campaign, as the principal was still employed on that date.

Under CPS policy, any time a principal is fired, in emergency situations the network office can temporarily replace them with an interim principal or the aforementioned AIC. In either situation, the LSC or ALSC chooses this principal. Due to a caveat in the difference between LSCs (direct-election power) and ALSCs (advisory/recommendation voting to the district), the central office (by way of the local network) made an executive decision to remove our principal for whatever undisclosed reason. Knowing that the ALSC had just hired the principal, it was known that this would be met with contention from its members. Making the principal's firing part of an emergency situation made it easier to transition a person who would do the bidding of central office. Making the firing four days before the first day of school would make this process smoother for the central office, but more chaotic for students, teachers, and families at SOJO.

The first decision of the interim principal (Ms. Jackson's replacement) was to drop the schedule that was agreed on for the year. Although an incomprehensible decision to make four days before the first day of school, teachers and students were outraged. Many students had participated in reading intensive and Advanced Placement (AP) prep courses in the summer and were preparing to get their college applications in order for early submission. To have this process obliterated in one fell swoop was devastating for students and teachers. Five months of work was taken away without any consultation. Where there was no real explanation or claim to criminal activity by the principal, the confusion around her firing rapidly oscillated our emotions between confusion, hurt, anger, and rage. Responding to the interim's decisions, students participated in a sit-in on the second day of school, protesting the dropping of their schedules. To publicize the sit-in, a few high school students posted a YouTube video of a brief moment in the protest, gaining support throughout the city.

In solidarity with the teaching staff and students, I attended a meeting with Alderman Munoz following classes on the second day of school. We made a request to meet with central office, but the alderman replied that in his conversations with central office, they alerted him that due to personnel concerns (i.e., CPS's liability concerning any violation of the principal's privacy) they could not discuss the rationale for the principal's firing. For all of us that came to the alderman's office, this was an obvious sign that they had no real reason for her firing. As our conversation progressed, we also alerted the alderman that the firing of SOJO's principal set a precedent, and closings around the city took a similar route. In two years prior, a set of high schools in the city that were either closed or consolidated. Since the emergence of Renaissance 2010, CPS closures have come in the form of phase-out (when a school stops accepting freshmen and closes after the last group of students graduate), direct closure (when an actual school building is closed), or turnaround (the administration and staff are fired, with the fired staff having the opportunity to reapply). As witness to all of these particular closures/turnaround, we were concerned that SOJO would be next in line to be consolidated. The dropping of the schedule only added fuel to the fire as wholesale curricular change appeared to prime us for closure.

Where we didn't get a firm commitment from the alderman to support our challenge to central office, we agreed to keep each other abreast of any new issues or concerns that came our way. After leaving his office, we briefly convened outside to discuss the next steps in terms of the immediate concerns of the school. Included in these next steps were meeting with the ALSC and keeping the teachers abreast of what we were hearing from either of our interactions with CPS or the new administration. In the back of our minds, however, was the opportunity for CPS to finally consolidate the campuses, using whatever rationale they could use. Years earlier, central office alerted the four campuses that small schools were too expensive to maintain, especially with four separate administrations and a team of specialists in each school.

Further complicating the matter was the fact that UNO had expressed interest in taking over SOJO's portion of the campus on numerous occasions. In a speech on public schooling at the Chicago Union Club, UNO CEO Rangel commended the newly appointed principal on taking matters into her own hands in a "difficult situation." Though his comments were not central to our concerns, it still compounded all the issues we had to contend with in the immediate chaos.

During the second week of school, SOJO's interim principal decided to have a parent meeting explaining what happened during the first week of school. Due to a barrage of parents calling SOJO's main office and coming to the school in person, CPS supported the interim principal in addressing community concerns through a large format. Interestingly enough, the newly appointed principal had no experience as an administrator and none in facilitating a large community meeting with parents, students, teachers, staff, and community members that were highly upset. To offer "support" in this effort, central office brought the administration from the network (the geographic region where SOJO resides—we were part of the West Side Network) to address any concerns. In attendance was the network chief, the network director of instruction and assessment, the network community and family liaison, and a host of other officials. As spectacle, the sight of all of these relatively young Black and Latino/a central office officials instantly reminded me as to how White supremacy works in big city "hot button" issues (in this case education). The hope of CPS, by bringing officials who were people of color, was to hopefully quell the discontent of the audience. The thought is that if Black and Latino/a parents see people like themselves as leadership in the central office, they might feel proud and go easy on them. Fortunately, members of the SOJO community did not succumb to the attempt to pacify their concerns.

The meeting began with network officials introducing themselves. The newly appointed principal had the responsibility of explaining what was happening with the turn of events at SOJO. Since her appointment, hosts of students were still without schedules. In the attempt to address the new scheduling system, students were placed in classes they had taken years before, or in classes that had never been taught at the school. Teachers were unable to create preps (lesson plans, unit plans, activities, etc.) for courses created in SOJO's first week. Removed from the schedule were honors and AP courses, for which students had been attending summer "boot camps" to prepare them for the challenges of the classes. The fact that none of this was taken into account when the classes were canceled was enough to make students, teachers, and families irate. Compounding this series of events was the fact that there was no consultation by the new principal with the ALSC, teachers, or the central office as to what the best strategy for the transition would be.

The new principal continued to explain in the meeting that there were some performance issues that needed to be addressed immediately in the school. Changing the schedule, despite its ill-advised timing, was the attempt to address the issues at hand. By the new principal's account, SOJO's math and reading scores were not up to par with the district standards. Taking a snapshot of the math and reading data, the interim principal failed to acknowledge what was happening in the data longitudinally. This became more evident in her report to students, families and staff.

In the public comment section of the meeting, I offered a question to the new principal and the network staff regarding the data. I explained that I wasn't offering this question as someone who was a member of the design team, a member of the ALSC, or someone who is a volunteer social studies teacher at the school. I was asking my question as someone who is a professor of educational policy studies who also studies issues of school equity for a living. If the longitudinal data is demonstrating an upward trend, why was the principal fired? According to CPS standards, she was doing her job. Additionally, why would a schedule be dropped two days before the start of school to accommodate these concerns? After about five seconds of silence, one of the network officials answered by giving me his name and a phone number where he could be reached. Understanding his answer as insufficient, he said that it was all he could offer at the moment. After their inability to answer the question, they sent another person from the network (a young Latina) who gave me their card with an offer to contact her office, which was "really concerned about the issues I raised." Again, the hope was to quell my concerns by extending the professional courtesy of providing me with her information.

Adding to the network's follies, the interim principal's ineptitude was further revealed as students, families, staff, and community members testified to the chaos and destabilization the recent changes brought to SOJO. Students spoke to parents explaining that they couldn't get the classes they registered for. Teachers testified that in addition to courses being canceled, book orders were not made and some classes were without supplies. At one point the interim even offered to purchase iPads for teachers with the money not used to purchase the requested supplies. Community members testified that all of the current happenings speak to a citywide attempt to destabilize schools that were actually moving in the right direction. Members of the LSC testified that the events of the last couple of weeks were out of compliance with CPS protocol. From this point on the Rewind to August 9 campaign was in full swing.

Reflecting on their sit-in and testimonies at the public hearing, students staged a community march on the Friday of the week of the community meeting. Through their efforts, they were able to galvanize students from other local schools, members of the Chicago Teachers Union (CTU), and concerned community members, including members from the original hunger strikers. The march traveled throughout La Villita, garnering support from local residents and onlookers. Interesting to this protest was the fact that it was student led and family supported. Students contacted their peers through social media while parents joined in support of the students. This is important throughout the ordeal as this becomes a key element in the community's response.

The weeks following the community forum were filled with the barrage of calamities, highlighting destabilization through benign neglect. Most notably utilized in the language of urban renewal, benign neglect in the case of school destabilization comes in the form of eradicating school infrastructure and existing practices. From an administrative standpoint, removing a principal from such a critical moment in the school year makes it impossible to engage the subtle nuances needed to build relationships with students and families. Because the interim appeared initially to have no interest in said relationships, the beginning of the year was marked with a host of fights between students and a considerable number of students transferring to other schools. Worst off were the freshmen, rendered unable to come to know SOJO as a place of learning. Instead, their introduction was to a place starting to slowly unravel.

During these nine weeks destabilization operates as a multilayered phenomenon that also took place during one the largest acts of public resistance by organized labor in almost twenty-five years in Chicago. By the same token, coupling SOJOs destabilization with the CTU strike of 2012 allowed Chicagoans outside the neighborhoods of Little Villita and North

Lawndale to gain a deeper understanding of the inner workings of CPS at numerous levels. From one perspective, the idea of a teachers union reframing their strike to protest the current trend of neoliberal corporate education reform, the events at SOJO became yet another space for residents around the city to understand the depth of central office dysfunction. Simultaneously, current situation at SOJO would operate as a micro example of the attempt to remove critical material and human resources from the system.

Deepening the destabilization, CPS decided to fire two of the founding members of SOJO's teaching staff (Katie Hogan and Angela Sangha-Gadsen). Using the veil of "personnel issues," both teachers were told they were removed for "performance issues." Both Katie and Angela were summoned to the principal office after eighth period. Both were told that their positions were being "redefined." The principal then proceeded to read them a letter from the central office, alerting them that if they had any further questions to contact the network or central office. Because the interim principal knew how popular these teachers were with students, it was strategic to have them removed at the end of the school day. Because there are always students in their classrooms after school, news spread like wildfire of their removal. As the "redefinition" rationale sounded dubious at best, both teachers consulted with the teachers union to get at the bottom of their removal. A former SOJO teacher who took a job with the CTU informed Katie and Angela that the school was engaging in a process of "redefining" two positions at the school. Because the original class schedule was dropped, the interim principal had the ability to redefine positions to fit the newly assigned courses. Because a CTU teacher cannot be terminated without a hearing and other subsequent actions, principals often use the strategy of redefiniton, forcing a mandatory removal of the existing teacher because they often don't have the proper certification for the redefined position. Understanding that it was their right as employees to know the reason of their termination, both Katie and Angela remained proactive in their pursuit of justice in their current employment predicament. Coupled with the efforts of the CTU, their pursuit revealed that they were both qualified for the redefined positions. Due to this concerted effort from CTU attorneys, combined with the support of students, parents, and fellow staff members, they were able to resume their positions at SOJO.

Adding further to the chaos, our counselor/social worker was removed due to an enrollment requirement. At the time, CPS had a requirement that schools must have at least 363 students in order to employ a social worker. During SOJO's destabilization, the enrollment was 362 students. At SOJO, the social worker is critical to our process in that this is the person responsible for coordinating any external resources students may need ranging from mental health support to summer internships to employment opportunities. As a crucial member of SOJO's faculty, she was often first responder to students who were dealing with particular challenges at home. Her ability to locate reliable spaces and organizations that could address students' needs is an invaluable resource in making sure small schools are run effectively.

As the ALSC, we decided the best approach was to hold CPS to their policy of having the decision to fire a principal rest with the council. Despite only having advisory power, we were heavily consulted by the network in the selection of the administrator in charge and our principal in the previous school year. The fact that they complied with our recommendation so easily in the first two instances brought serious concern to the council. In previous interactions with the network, we were guaranteed that they would respect the decisions of the district. The most recent decision to fire our principal was completely out of character with their most recent behavior. Still hiding behind the "personnel" violation, we felt that it would be the hardest to get a direct answer as to why our principal was fired. However, we did feel if we pushed the district on their inability to follow process, we had the chance to retain our principal and the courses scheduled to be taught that year.

Some of the ALSC members reminded us of how important it was to get students, parents, and teachers outside the council engaged in the process. It took a concerted effort to galvanize the resources of the aforementioned groups to develop clarity on what our demands were as the Rewind to August 9th campaign. This required talking to multiple factions of the central office, figuring out the best strategies available to make sure our demands were met. As a democratic process, this was quite messy in that it called for members of multiple groups to coordinate meetings to decide the next steps moving forward. Because there were not warring factions within our group, the most substantial challenges were often logistical and deciding on action steps.

One of the first meetings was held at Patricia (Patty) Buenrostro's house. Present were students, parents, teachers, and concerned community members. Members of the ALSC organized other parents to come. Students organized themselves to be in attendance, while teachers organized among themselves to ensure representation at the meeting. Throughout the process of the destabilization, meetings such as these were critical in galvanizing the community's ability to resist the will of CPS. Showing their continued support, members of CTU were also present, offering assistance when needed.

Due to sheer numbers and pleasant weather, the first meeting was in Patty's backyard. Here was where the initial discussion and planning of the student march was held, along with the initial plans to meet with central office. Like the majority of in-school meetings, our gathering was translated, making sure there was accountability to the parents who primarily speak Spanish. Additionally, we were also able to have an introductory conversation on the demands of the Rewind campaign.

From Patty's backyard we were able plan future meetings to solidify and execute the strategy of getting the Rewind demands met. This included public meetings at neighborhood spaces, including Veterans of Foreign Wars (VFW) meeting halls, public libraries, and Patty's house. Similar to the initial hunger strike, meetings were supported and attended by the myriad community and labor organizations (e.g., CTU, ENLACE Chicago, etc.), along with local residents from North Lawndale and La Villita.

From the backyard and house meetings at Patty's, organizing shifted to ALSC meetings. Since the community forum at the high school, the newly appointed principal began to isolate herself, limiting contact with students, parents, community members, and the ALSC. A new policy was instituted at SOJO where an appointment was mandatory to get a meeting from the newly appointed principal. Where illegal under CPS policies, the tactic was used to develop some sense of control of the situation. Because there was such discontent with the current moment at the school, the new principal probably felt as if she had no choice. As an ALSC, our demands to the network created a situation in which we seemed to be having meetings two to three times per week. Being an ALSC member, I began to think about everyone working at SOJO, trying to grasp the level of fatigue people were experiencing. Beginning work anytime between 6:45 and 7:00 a.m., and attending meetings that ended anywhere between 9:00 and 9:30 p.m., the experience begun to tax the body and mind. Because I wasn't teaching at the school, with the fatigue I was feeling, I could only imagine what it was feeling like for students and staff. Nevertheless, the group moved forward, remaining intent on the demands of our campaign.

Throughout the process we noticed an unusual strategy by the head of the network and other member of central office. Because they knew I was employed at the university, they would often try to speak to me after the meetings, expressing their opinion about what was actually happening in the district. After numerous denials that the firing of our principal was an attempt to consolidate the four schools, our conversation would quickly turn into how they were attempting to assist the school in reaching its goals. Once I would alert the ALSC of this strategy, we thought that we should use it as a tactic to potentially understand the long-term plans for the school. From this space we requested two meetings with the network chief. The first meeting I would have with her by myself. The second meeting would be with her, parents, and ALSC members. The point of this strategy was to let the district know that not only did we have a committed set of parents and students willing to fight for the school, it would also be difficult for the district to present a rationale for closing the school given this upward-trending data.

My meeting with the network chief was early in the morning at her office. The parents and ALSC members were scheduled to meet with her later that afternoon. I began the conversation with the fact that I knew I could not discuss our principal's situation or the dismissal of Katie and Angela due to personnel confidentiality issues. However, what I wanted to understand was how, as an ALSC, we could not think that the network was moving to close us. The response was an emphatic denial of the network and district's attempt to close us. Since the inception of Renaissance 2010, over one hundred schools had been closed or "turned around," where the entire administration and staff were fired and replaced by a new group. The rationale was that budget shortfalls, coupled with declining student populations created a situation where schools were either "underutilized" or in a state of chronic failure. By the network chief's account, this was not the case with SOJO. In fact, it was emphasized that it was one of the places where things were done "right," and served as a model for the rest of the district. I responded if that was the case, then why all the chaos at the beginning of the year? If things were being done "right," then why would an interim be placed in the school two days before the first day of school? Second, why would she at the outset decide to drop *all* of the courses and assign new ones without warning? Customary to our conversations, the answer wasn't enough to gauge how much was accurate, but the decisions of the interim principal were referred to as "rookie mistakes." The answer was unacceptable. It was careless to place the lives of students in flux in this matter. With October approaching, college applications were due. In some instances, the courses needed for acceptance to some colleges and universities were removed, placing students in jeopardy. Placing a new administrator under these conditions was irresponsible and short-sighted. When asked about a plan from the network to rectify the situation, the reply was that the network promised to work with the school to get the situation "under control."

Unfortunately the later meeting with the parents and ALSC members was no less fruitful. When we reported back to each other, the sentiment was that the network was in no shape or form willing or prepared to respond to our needs. For these reasons, we would have to expand our efforts to go directly to the CPS central office and speak during the monthly public board meeting. This was the best way to get our story to the district. The network consistently proved to be inept in addressing our concerns.

CPS public board hearings are notorious for their length and inability to get responses from the board. Because board members are appointed by the mayor, many are out of touch with the educational concerns of Black and Brown families from communities, who bear the brunt of the three Ds. Understanding this from the outset, we also engaged in a media strategy to contact local newspapers, alerting them of our story. We also let them know that we would be available to speak to them after the board hearing. To our advantage was the fact that CPS, by way of the network violated its own policy in the removal of our principal and two teachers.

In order to get on the public speaking list, participants need to be present at the central office at six a.m. to sign up for speaking at the public commentary portion of the board meeting. The meeting is usually held in late morning or early afternoon, most notably at a time that is completely inaccessible to working families. At the same rate, we planned so two of the ALSC members could get to CPS headquarters at six a.m. to get on the sign-up list.

The meeting was filled with the pomp and circumstance of board meetings. Schools that were doing well were individually recognized, along with students from particular schools who were either randomly chosen or part of a boutique program in the district. Public commentary is held at the end, in what comes off as a diversionary tactic by the board. Race and class are heavily at play in these moments, as the issues and concerns expressed in the public commentary portion of the meeting are usually by people of color from low-income/working-class communities exhibiting the most extreme examples of disinvestment and marginalization.

When two of our ALSC members spoke, one gave her testimony in Spanish (Mrs. Rojas-Garcia), while Patty translated. Both explained how our principal was fired, how our classes were dropped, and we currently were short on supplies. We reminded the district that the events of the first month of school were in direct violation of CPS policies regarding the removal of school leadership. In their allotted two minutes, Patty and Mrs. Rojas-Garcia continued to explain how this is having severe effects on students who are both entering SOJO as freshmen and beginning their senior year.

Interestingly enough, the response from the board was very unusual. Earlier in the day, there was a press conference held by a coalition of community organizations that have been in a extended fight with the board, holding them accountable to their implementation of the three Ds. Because of the contentious relationship, they are usually greeted with rolling eyes from board members and other CPS attendees. In the end, however, their efforts have been instrumental in publicizing the practices of CPS that continue to contribute to the marginalization of certain communities by way of education. We expected a similar response. Anticipating the usual "thank you" and subsequent silence from board members, the CEO (Jean Claude Brizzard) and chief education officer (Barbara Byrd-Bennett) responded that they had no knowledge of the events we spoke of. Both looked extremely surprised as Patty and Mrs. Rojas-Garcia finished their testimony. Even stranger, they asked for our contact information and promised to reach out to us. Once we left the room, representatives from the newspaper we contacted greeted us and interviewed Patty and Mrs. Rojas-Garcia on the spot. Simultaneously, there was also a group of women hovering around us with cellular phones, appearing to record all of the conversation. Rico Gutstein alerted me that this was the media department of CPS. The head of media relations was also in the hallway and attempted to defend their intrusive behavior of the women as only "doing their jobs." Again, the policing and perpetual surveillance of Black and Brown bodies create hostility to give CPS the excuse to rescind their efforts.

Nevertheless, we continued our process and met as the ALSC to strategize our next steps. The response from Brizzard and Byrd-Bennett, while surprising, was good. The issue was to continue to pressure on the district, since the network hadn't produced the results we anticipated. We gave them a week to contact us. If they didn't do so in a week, we would follow up with their office to see what was happening.

Throughout this process, my role as a university professor appeared to bring about some type of cache. To members of the network and to the newly appointed principal, I was seen as an insider of sorts, a quasi-voice of reason due to my employment as a university professor. It was strange to me in that I am rarely positioned as the voice of reason. Usually I'm the person who's not invited to meetings and events with the district because of what is thought to be noncompliant behavior. But for the purposes of getting the Rewind goals met, I had no problem with occupying that space momentarily.

The newly appointed principal seemed to have this view of me during the whole ordeal. After weeks of heated ALSC meetings that included the network, parents, and students, she felt as if she was being attacked from all fronts. Viewing me as the "reasonable" member of the ALSC, she requested to meet with me individually. At first I was skeptical of the request, in that this is a common tactic often used by school administrators and central office officials to see if they can appeal to your "humanistic side," with the hope of lessening the antagonism toward them in future meetings. I discussed this with other members of the ALSC, but they felt that it would be good to meet with her individually, with the purpose of her understanding where we were coming from as an ALSC and to gather more information about rehiring Ana Herrera as our counselor.

We met just before the beginning of first period. After the exchange of pleasantries, she began to explain to me the process of her hiring as the interim principal. She said she was approached by the network and was told there was an opening at a local school. They told her the data was bad and they were in desperate need of drastic measures to rectify the situation. When she saw the data, her first response was that she couldn't understand why we had students in honors and AP classes when their grade point averages were so low. From her viewpoint, it appeared as if students needed more remedial support. Unbeknownst to her was the fact that the instructional support she saw as necessary was being offered to the students who were in the honors and AP courses. I explained to her that the boot camps and summer assignments were specifically created to provide students with the support they needed not only for exams, but for continued skill development. Because the network only gave her the previous year's data, she didn't pay attention to the fact that the school was actually improving according to the performance metrics issued by the state and CPS. She presented me with a letter from the CPS central office stating that we had too few students to retain a counselor and the position had to be removed.

Without approaching her antagonistically, I began to see clearly that she had been pawned by the network and central office. Though I didn't know if she had volunteered for the pawning or was duped, her leadership style informed me that it appeared to be a combination of the two. Her practice of insulating herself from faculty, students, and parents was short-sighted and resulted in further marginalization of the SOJO community. With the help of the network, she was instantly positioned as the enemy of SOJO. For these reasons this became the moment to inform her about the political economy of Chicago and CPS, making it directly tangible to the current situation at SOJO. I began to explain to her that since its opening, SOJO has always been positioned as too expensive by the district. From opening day many felt that the school should be consolidated and that too many resources were spent on a neighborhood public school. I continued to explain that the current effort to consolidate the school comes by way of leadership shifts that allows the network to declare the school unstable and in need of an overhaul. This led to me explain that CPS's current budget austerity rhetoric (by way of cuts) allowed them to further marginalize communities they deemed unworthy of necessary resources. Not knowing if she had any allegiances to UNO or Juan Rangel, I continued to explain that this is how charters have become the new trend. The district finds them to be cheap substitutes for neighborhood schools, while starving existing public schools of students and resources they would originally receive. If there are no students, the school is deemed "underutilized" and is subsequently closed or consolidated. I also explained that UNO and a number of charter networks have their eye on SOJO. If SOJO were to close, the self-fulfilling prophecy would be in full motion. Her single-word response to this was "Fuck." She knew she was in the eye of the storm, but I'm not sure if she knew how engulfed she was in the chaos. The meeting concluded with her stating that she understood my points, and that she would move on them accordingly.

Following with the needs of the campaign, we followed up with the central office after we didn't hear from them for a week. They responded by setting an appointment with us in the following week. When we convened as the ASLC/Rewind campaign, we decided to send a group of parents (Patty Buenrostro, Mrs. Mendez, Ms. Josso, and Mrs. Garcia-Rojas) and the teacher member of the ALSC (Yamali Rodriguez). All were comfortable in telling the story to Brizzard and reaffirming that our rights as an ALSC had been violated and were not in concert with the way the network conducted procedure in our most recent principal selection.

The report-back to the ALSC and the Rewind members alerted us that the both Brizzard and Byrd-Bennett were receptive to our concerns and responded with shock and awe at the situation. SOJO was not on any warning list (either for probation or closure) and had upward-trending data. For us, this substantiated our assumption that the network chief acted without approval from district office. Without going into a back-and-forth argument with CPS, our concern was with what could be done to rectify the situation. They said they would respond immediately, first by appointing two officials from LSC relations to oversee the process of getting our principal back to SOJO.

With its usual knack for drama, the timing of our meeting was also interesting in that we found ourselves in the throes of revolving door CPS leadership. Shortly after the meeting with members of the ALSC, Brizzard resigned, citing that the process of getting schools on track became too much about him and not enough about the students. Despite what this rhetoric might mean, it was good that we had Barbara Byrd-Bennett (then chief educational officer) in the room, as she replaced Brizzard as chief executive officer. Due to the continuity of both officials being present, we were able to follow up with her office in case there were any future issues.

At this point it appeared as if we were gaining some momentum. The network chief appeared to be out of the picture, but now we had to deal with the two officials from the Department of LSC relations to get our principal back. Now the issue became whether or not the ALSC could engage in a democratic process to ensure that the needs of the Rewind" campaign were met. For the remainder of our process, the majority of the endeavor would take place in the ALSC meetings, as the two CPS officials were high-ranking employees in LSC relations.

For the entire duration, morale at the school continued to decline, though some of the fighting among students declined, and student transfers also began to slow. Nevertheless, some classes still were without supplies while teachers found themselves at wit's end, without the necessary materials or support to teach effectively. SOJO seniors were still without the critical support they needed as college application dates loomed near. Even though Angela and Katie got their jobs back, it was a process of being displaced for almost three weeks and returning to a chaotic environment. Luckily, strong, preexisting relationships with students were able to bring some level of peace of mind. Like students and teachers, parents were also fatigued and upset. Now we were in our fifth week of pushing back on the district with minimum results regarding the Rewind campaign. The process began to wear on all of us, but with the network out of the way, we were able to envision a process that would allow us to meet our goals.

Every ALSC meeting has a section for public comments. Because students, parents, and ALSC members had become so embattled with the process of running into dead ends with the network, frustrations were often vented with the interim principal during public comment session. The fact of having two officials from LSC relations didn't seem to help much at first, but their direct contact with central administration proved useful in the end. Again, my position as an academic seemed to allow some leeway in terms of having conversations with them. Both had expressed to me that they were impressed to see a younger person in academia involved in community-driven efforts. It also allowed me to access information that would prove useful to our efforts. Nevertheless, by this time we were in our sixth week of school. Teachers were still without critical supplies, our counselor had not been rehired, and students (especially our seniors applying for college) were growing ever more restless by the second.

During the ALSC meeting of the seventh week of the ordeal, we were visited by the head of LSC relations. Due to the persistent efforts of the parents, students, and teachers, administrators at the central office finally came through on their promise. His presentation to the ALSC and the parents in attendance was confusing at first, but being embattled in political-speak left us with the idea that good things were to come. In his comments he let us know that Barbara Byrd-Bennett had paid attention to our concerns, and we could engage in a process to replace the interim principal. What he did not say, however, was whether or not our previous principal would be eligible to apply for her job.

In Chicago, in order to apply for a principal position, you have to go through an eligibility process. This includes a battery of tests and assessments that makes you "principal eligible." Since our principal was dubiously fired, we were unsure as to whether or not her eligibility would be revoked. When pressed on this issue, he just assured us that the decision of the CEO would be to our liking. Even in a side conversation with him he wouldn't reveal whether or not our principal would be eligible, but hinted that we would be satisfied with the decision.

One week later, members of the ALSC were alerted that our principal would be eligible. Our responsibility as a council was now to approve a listing to be posted in the CPS job announcements and field applications as they came in. Luckily, because we were in the seventh week of school, we had few applicants for the position. With our principal in the applicant pool, we could engage in a process that could get one of our Rewind demands met. Outside of the ALSC meetings, the sentiment was that CPS needed to respect our process and let any other matters be handled among the faculty, staff, and students.

In discussions outside of ALSC meetings with students, faculty, and parents, there seemed to be a sense of relief. Despite the fact that our principal was declared eligible, there was also a lingering sense of fatigue. The chaos of the day-to-day continued to wear on staff and students, while parents remained dissatisfied with the interim principal's struggles to manage SOJO effectively. During this time the ALSC meetings were handled masterfully by our parent-president, Sandra Mendez, who had experience working in CPS and as a longtime member of another local LSC as a staff member. The combination of her inputs, along with the support of new parent members (Ms. Josso and Mrs. Rojas-Garcia holding the interim principal and CPS officials accountable), as well as the seasoned veterans on the ALSC (Shirley Jones and Patty Buenrostro) were critical in developing a space to complete the task of getting our demands met.

Because the officials from the division of LSC relations were with us throughout the second half of the process, they also alerted us on how to make sure that all our requirements were up to date. This included new trainings for new ALSC members, including principal hiring, budget, and voting rules. Because the ALSC had to deal with the upheaval of the first eight weeks, the trainings took a backseat to our immediate concerns. Nevertheless, we were able to complete the necessary trainings.

In the ninth week, we finally held our ALSC meeting that would decide a process to replace the current interim. During the meeting we approved the announcement and had public comment (no one participated during this public comment section). Luckily for us, our elected principal was the only principal who submitted an application (most "principal-eligible" applicants have taken positions by the eighth week of the school year). As an ALSC we approved her application for admission and her subsequent rehiring. The main demand for the Rewind to August 9 was met.

In Reflection: Collateral Damage and Recovery

Despite our victory in our circumstantial replay of the struggle similar to the one to get the high school open, there was still much to be taken care of. We just endured nine weeks of maddening chaos. Now our responsibility was to recoup the damage incurred in the process. Despite our fatigue, our victory provided us a smidgeon of uplift. There was still much work to be done and very little time in which to do it. The beginning of our freshman class introduction to high school had been compromised while our seniors were scrambling to align their work to graduate and move toward life beyond SOJO.

Our recuperation process included the getting some of the lost courses back, while getting support from the network to purchase supplies originally scheduled to be ordered at the beginning of the school year. We were able to rehire our counselor, but we still needed to shift our schedule to resemble the one we originally planned for in the beginning of the year.

In the strangest turn of events, at a November ALSC meeting, CPS and the Network delivered a banner to SOJO, recognizing the school for having the highest gains in the West Side Network. After nine weeks of insanity from the network, they went back to the original data and affirmed our initial refusal of the network's excuse to remove our principal. Still in fact, the ridiculousness is emblematic of what can happen to schools if there is not a concerted effort to fight back. Similar to other localized efforts in Chicago (e.g., Altgeld Gardens, Pilsen, etc.) and large efforts in major cities (e.g., New Orleans, New York, Philadelphia, Newark, Oakland, Los

Angeles, etc.), the SOJO example provides a glimpse into the organizational irrationality of large school districts.

Hidden under the guise of "personnel issues" and "central office procedure," the first ten weeks of the 2012–2013 school year stand as a quintessential example of how, if left unchecked, central office officials can orchestrate a series of events that serve personal interests while leaving students and families in flux. As Critical Race Praxis, the ability to work collaboratively in highly contested space operates as the necessary pretext to galvanize educational justice efforts through neighborhood/family networks, teacher unions, and community organizations. Pushing the construct of less time with abstract theorizing and more time on the ground, the original tenets of the hunger strike were revisited as the community again saw the need to challenge CPS policy as critical to the survival of the school.

The messiness of struggle tethered by the political economy of race and class do not account for sanguine, safe, and smooth transitions in leadership. Coupled with the commitment from the central office to destabilize the ability of SOJO to solidify efforts to ensure effective quality education, it becomes important to recognize tensions at the ground level that can compound the attempt to challenge corporate, neoliberal rationales. At the same time, it should not discourage us from engaging work in a way that remains responsible to community concerns. In the field of battle, allies are sometimes lost, but several are gained if we continue to remain responsible. For my particular situation, I cannot make the claim that all of our actions we're correct in engaging the moving target of CPS. Instead, I must be responsible with regard for the mistakes made in the process that perpetually has the potential to place the school in jeopardy of closing. Being positioned as the voice of reason in the struggle, while strange to me, was a gendered and classed position due to the assumptions about my occupation of university professor.

At the same time I remain confident in the community members and teachers who remain at SOJO. There will definitely be future struggles ahead, but I am trustful that the students and families of Little Village and North Lawndale will not surrender to the powers that be. In our praxis we must remain responsible for our victories and mistakes while embracing a commitment to make them nonetheless. Because this work is intimately tied to the life and death of community-centered public education as we know it, I remain willing to work in solidarity with those concerned with creating quality, viable schools for young people and their families. It is a struggle that I am honored to take part in. With that blessing, I know the struggles ahead will present challenges that will call for a similar commitment.

Epilogue

Educational Justice in Troubling Times

> We made some strides . . . but in the long scheme of things were they significant? . . . I hope so . . . I don't think we'll find out for another few years when those first couple of classes get out there and do some things. I feel like that's gonna be our true . . . that's when we're gonna know.
>
> —Ida Joyce Sia, interview

The give and take of school creation is intense. For every gain, there are often multiple losses or compromises that have the opportunity to take the group further away from the original intentions of community struggle. In the uneven, contested, and maligned fight for educational justice, there was is much gained and much that is sacrificed. In the end, SOJO is a different place from what it was in the fall of 2005. For all intents and purposes it's supposed to be. The question that must perpetually be revisited is *to what extent are the views and values set forward by the original community-driven effort reflected in the day-to-day realities of the school?* By our own assessment, the results are mixed, seasoned with the myriad moral victories that don't show up in school data reports.

> Like with anything, when you have so much turnover and there's not enough effort in keeping the history alive and the original mission alive, people forget or people are not involved in the fact that this school was born out of struggle and this was not just about quality education but community empowerment and a lot of that has been lost. (Jaime De Leon interview, August 8, 2012)

Under these circumstances, the idea is not to wax nostalgic about the "good ol' days," but to actively plan and prepare for the new set of challenges under neoliberal corporate education reform. Zizek (2011) talks about living in the "end" times, but not as an argument for total dystopia. Instead, I understand his comments as speaking to the fact that this new era presents us with something we have never witnessed. Of course, the converging policies of corporations and the state is nothing new. However, the current dynamics are such that the intensity of the moment has widened economic and social disparities almost to the point of no return. And old moment is not only *ending*, but a new moment is *beginning*. The main concern however, is that we don't know what this new moment entails.

At the same time, one should not feel that all is lost. Instead, it is important to gage the numerous contradictions of our existence in the struggle for educational justice. SOJO, as a school that is not absent of said contradictions, is a space to be understood instead of romanticized. From one perspective, the community got a $63 million building in a low-income/working-class, densely populated community. Conversely, the four schools are often under threat of consolidation, under the rhetoric that they are too expensive and best operate as a comprehensive high school. Jaime De Leon's sentiment is one that speaks to the necessity of understanding the days ahead.

> We've been hearing those rumblings since the first year. And it's like unfortunately, what's going to be our response if they make the announcement (to consolidate) tomorrow? We're going to have to get back in reaction mode versus having some sort of unity inside the school that's representative of all the schools and is ready to act. (Jaime De Leon interview, August 8, 2012)

In the specific case of SOJO, there have been four administrations in nine years (five if we count the administrator in charge). Yet, we also have the largest representation of founding teachers of any school in the multiplex. At the time of printing, SOJO will have graduated its sixth class with almost 70 percent of the students pursuing higher education. Contrasting this point, we have been on academic probation twice in nine years that we have been open. Further adding to the contradictions, we have also been recognized for having the highest gains in our regional network and recognized by the state board of education (ISBE) for membership in top-125 achieving high schools in the state. From a critical perspective, all of the accolades and sanctions are reflective of an arbitrary numbers game centered in a particular articulation of achievement data.

There still hasn't been a total inclusion of the residents of North Lawndale. Currently, the African-American population in any of the four schools oscillates between 2 percent and 15 percent. Where physical confrontations have quelled to an extent, there are still moments when tensions flare between African-American and Latino/a students. African-American students continue to talk about how they feel as if the school is only for Mexicans. Despite herculean efforts to recruit students from North Lawndale, the current onslaught of charters in the community makes the task incredibly challenging.

The fight not to become a "regular school" is not an aberration. At every given moment we are challenged by some central office policy that usually limits the ability of young people to think and create. Because these are not new gripes, they can quickly become tired and damming. A colleague reminds me that we cannot offer a collective eulogy to public schools when so many lives are in the balance. I agree with her point. Instead of trying to strike a balance between the disparaging and the victories, I try to think about it in terms of understanding the current educational landscape. Tiffany Childress reminded me of the necessity of collectively fighting through the fatigue of challenging state power.

> You get tired . . . you gotta keep fighting for it because the people in power already have an agenda for it. In order for you to have a different orientation for the space you gotta keep fighting for it. A base of people could keep it sustained, but the base gets divided. (Tiffany Childress interview, July 31, 2012)

For many communities, the fight for quality neighborhood public schools is real. Not only in Chicago, but New Orleans, Philadelphia, Los Angeles, Newark, Houston, Detroit, and Oakland, California have been bombarded with charters that play on the desperation of families yearning for quality schools. Despite the facade of new lockers and refurbished hallways, what some families are getting is worse than what they had before. A culture of hyper-high-stakes testing has made for the rationale of removing students who may struggle with assessments designed to demonstrate how well a student takes a test. As those who have historically received the least are being left with even less, there is a tragic need for something more. Yamamoto and Andrade's call for hope to be supported materially is at an all time high.

SOJO does not exist in a vacuum. Instead, it is a school in a city that has closed or repurposed almost 150 schools since 2004. In one fell swoop, 49 schools were closed and/or repurposed in one summer, counting for the largest single set of school closings in the history of the United States. Chicago remains a hyperracialized, segregated, and politically entangled metropolis. To speak of it as anything else is falsely shrouding the real-life isolation, containment, and marginalization that takes place in African-American and Latino/a neighborhoods. Despite the devastation this has brought to some communities (state-sponsored violence in the form of gentrification, school closings, and displacement), residents have decided they will not take this lying down.

At an SOJO ALSC meeting on February 21, 2014, Patty Buenrostro challenged the committee with a set of questions that SOJO and other schools like it need to answer in perpetuity.

> How do we make sure we remain a school of Social Justice? What are our responsibilities to the mission and vision of the school? How does it move beyond ritual and becomes engrained in the permanent fabric of the school? (Field notes, February 21, 2014)

Another parent offered a similar account.

> Freshmen come to orientation and learn about the school, but they don't write anything down. There are no assignments to connect them to the larger struggle. They come to SOJO because it's the best option, but many don't really know why they're here. (ibid.)

My time at SOJO reminds me that in the age of neoliberal corporate education reform, community struggle for quality education will be in perpetuity. No matter how many awards SOJO receives, they do not save it from the sweeping rationale of the corporate state. The best strategy in the current moment is to model for other communities what is possible by maintaining transparency and collaboration with community members, while building capacity for the next struggle when (not if) it happens.

In the same vein, there is a strong sense of possibility in this political, social, and economic moment. The mayoral victories of Bill De Blasio in New York City and Ras Baraka in Newark, New Jersey have the promise of addressing decades of educational neglect in their respective locales. Teachers at Garfield High School in Seattle, Washington, sparked a movement to rid the city of an assessment that was wasting student's time throughout the district. Taking the cues from the CTU, a justice-minded slate called Union Power within United Teachers of Los Angeles (UTLA) has secured a recent victory in the August 29, 2014 election of new president Alex Caputo-Pearl. Similar to the format of the Caucus of Rank and File Educators (CORE) in the CTU, they used a slate that calls for an end to charter school proliferation, while raising community collaboration and the ending of exclusionary union policies that have isolated people of color from executive leadership (http://inthesetimes.com/working/entry/16700/los_angeles_alex_caputo_pearl).

Locally, teachers at Saucedo Academy in Chicago refused to administer the Illinois State Achievement Test (ISAT), sparking a citywide movement to challenge the existing order. Community members in the Mid-South region through the Kenwood Oakland Community Organization (KOCO) have revitalized an effort to save an existing neighborhood school (Walter Dyett High School). Taking a cue from community members in La Villita, a hunger strike is on the table as a way to bring attention to their struggles. Last, former SOJO teacher and current Blaine Elementary principal Troy Kamau LaRaviere issued a public letter to the mayor and CEO of CPS in a local newspaper regarding what it means to exist under the current regime of mayoral control.

> This administration gets away with this because we let them. We are the professionals. Yet, we allow political interests to dominate the public conversation about what's good for the children in our schools. Every time these officials misinform the public about the impact of their policies, we need to follow them with a press conference of our own to set the record straight . . . Those of us who know better must lift our voices to persuade the residents of Illinois to reject these backward ideas and to oust the politicians who peddle them. We must work together to build our own system-wide improvement effort. The future of public education is at stake, and the future of Chicago's children is at risk. We must lift our voices and be heard. (Letter to the editor, *Chicago Sun-Times*, May 9, 2014)

Sparking a citywide debate on the relevance of mayoral control, this effort, along with the aforementioned others, are indicative of the capacity to galvanize action for justice in serious times. LaRaviere is right: *this is not a drill.* We must get to work.

Glossary of Acronyms

AIC	administrator in charge
AIO	area instructional officer
ALSC	Advisory Local School Council
AMPS	Autonomous Management Program School
AP	Advanced Placement
AUSL	Academy of Urban School Leadership
CDC	Community Development Corporation
CEJE	Collaborative for Equity and Excellence in Education
CEO	chief executive officer, Chicago Public Schools
CEO2	chief educational officer, Chicago Public Schools
CHSRI	Chicago High School Redesign Initiative
CPS	Chicago Public Schools
Crib	Crib Collective
CRP	Critical Race Praxis
CRT	critical race theory
ETC	Education to Careers
ISBE	Illinois State Board of Education
KOCO	Kenwood Oakland Community Organization
LCDC	Lawndale Christian Development Corporation
LSC	Local School Council
LVCDC	Little Village Community Development Corporation
LVEJO	Little Village Environmental Justice Organization
NPIC	Nonprofit Industrial Complex
ONS	Office of New Schools
OPPD	Office of Principal Preparation and Development
Ren2010	Renaissance 2010
SOJO	Greater Lawndale High School for Social Justice
TAC	Transition Advisory Council
UNO	United Neighborhood Organization
VFW	Veterans of Foreign Wars

Bibliography

Ahmed-Ullah, N., and A. Richards (February 26, 2014). Charter school's expulsion rate vastly higher than rest of CPS. *Chicago Tribune.*

Alexander, M. (2010). *The new Jim Crow: Mass incarceration in the age of colorblindness.* New York: New Press.

Ancess, J. (2003). *Beating the odds: High schools as communities of commitment.* New York: Teachers College.

Anyon, J. (2005). *Radical possibilities: Public policy, urban education and a new social movement.* New York: Routledge.

Ayers, W., G. Ladson-Billings, G. Michie, and P. Noguera (eds.) (2008). *City kids, city schools: More reports from the front row.* New York: New Press.

Ayers, R., and W. Ayers (2011). *Teaching the taboo: Courage and imagination in the classroom.* New York: Teachers College.

Arrastia, L. (2007). Capital's daisy chain: Exposing Chicago's corporate coalition. *Journal of Critical Education Policy Studies* 5(1) (eric.ed.gov/?id=EJ839037).

Ball, S. J. (2007). *Education plc: Understanding private sector participation in public sector education.* New York: Routledge.

Bell, D. (1980). Brown v. board of education and the interest convergence dilemma. *Harvard Law Review* 93, 518–533.

Bell, D. (2008). *Race, racism and American law.* Aspen, CO: Aspen Publishers.

Bennett, L., J. Smith, and P. Wright, P. (eds.) (2006). *Where are poor people to live? Transforming Public Housing Communities.* London: M. E. Sharpe.

Boyd, M. R. (2008). *Jim Crow nostalgia: Reconstructing race in bronzeville.* Minneapolis, MN: University of Minnesota Press.

Brown, L., and E. Gutstein (2009, February 17). The charter difference: A comparison of Chicago charter and neighborhood high schools. *Collaborative for Equity and Justice in Education.*

Buras, K. L., J. Randels, and K. Y. Salaam. *Pedagogy, policy and the privatized city: Stories of dispossession and defiance from New Orleans.* New York: Teachers College.

Burch, P. (2009). *Hidden markets: The new education privatization.* New York: Routledge.

Camangian, P. (2011). Subverting the master('s) syllabus. *Monthly Review* 63(3), 128–135.

Cammarota, J., and A. Romero (eds.) (2014). *Raza studies: The public option for educational revolution.* Tucson: University of Arizona.

Cammarota, J., and M. Fine (eds.) (2008). *Revolutionizing education: Youth participatory action research in motion.* New York: Routledge.

Carter Andrews, D. J., and F. Tuitt (eds.) (2013). *Contesting the myth of a 'post racial' era: The continued significance of race in U.S. education.* New York: Peter Lang.

Civic Committee of the Commercial Club of Chicago (2003). Left Behind: Student achievement in Chicago's public schools. *Commercial Club of Chicago.*

Cortez, G. (2008). Education, politics, and a hunger strike: A social movement's struggle for education in Chicago's Little Village. Dissertation: University of Illinois at Urbana–Champaign.

Crenshaw, K., N. Gotanda, G. Peller, and K. Thomas (1995). *Critical race theory: The key writings that formed the movement.* New York: New Press.

Cutler, I. (2009). *Images of America: Chicago's Jewish west side.* Charleston, SC: Arcadia.

Delgago, R. (2003). Cross and blind alleys: A critical examination of recent writing about race. *Texas Law Review* 82(1), 121–152.

Delgado, R., and J. Stefancic (2001). *Critical race theory: An introduction.* New York: New York University Press.

Diamond, J. (1999). *Guns, germs and steel: The fates of human societies.* New York: W. W. Norton.

Dixson, A., and Rousseau, C. (2006). *Critical race theory in education: All God's children got a song.* New York: Routledge.

Duncan-Andrade, J. M. R. (2010). *What a coach can teach a teacher: Lessons urban schools can learn from a successful sports program.* New York: Peter Lang.

Duncan-Andrade, J. M. R. (2009). Note to educators: Hope required when growing roses in concrete. *Harvard Educational Review* 79(2), 1–13.

Duncan-Andrade, J. M. R., and E. Morrell (2008). *The art of critical pedagogy: Possibilities for moving from theory to practice in urban schools.* New York: Peter Lang.

Fabricant, M. (2010). *Organizing for educational justice: The campaign for public school reform in the south Bronx.* Minneapolis: University of Minnesota.

Fabricant, M., and M. Fine (2012). *Charter schools and the corporate makeover of public education: What's at stake?* New York: Teachers College.

Fortin, C. (November 15, 1998). Harrisons Steans biggest investment: Former banker works to make life better in Chicago's North Lawndale neighborhood. *Chicago Tribune.*

Freire, P. (1973). *Pedagogy of the oppressed.* New York: Continuum.

Freire, P. (2003). *Education for critical consciousness.* New York: Continuum.

Gillborn, D. (2008). *Racism and education: Coincidence or conspiracy?* New York: Routledge.

Ginwright, S. (2004). *Black in school: Afrocentric reform, urban youth, and the promise of hip-hop culture.* New York: Teachers College.

Ginwright, S., P. Noguera, and J. Cammarota (eds.) (2006). *Beyond resistance: Youth activism and community change—New democratic possibilities for practice and policy for America's youth.* New York: Routledge.

Ginwright, S. (2010). *Black youth rising: Activism and radical healing in urban America.* New York: Teachers College.

Glanton, D., W. Mullen, and A. Olivio (2011, February 18). Neighborhood population drain: Census shows central Chicago grew while outlying areas lost. *Chicago Tribune.*

Hackworth, J. (2007). *The neoliberal city: Governance, ideology and development in American urbanism.* Ithaca, NY: Cornell University Press.

Hale, C. R. (ed.) (2008). *Engaging contradictions: Theory, politics, and methods of activist scholarship.* Los Angeles: University of California.

Harris, C. (1993). Whiteness as property. *Harvard law review* 106(8), 1710–1791.

Harvey, D. (2009). *A brief history of neoliberalism.* London: Oxford University Press.

Hill, M. L. (2009). *Beats, rhymes and classroom life: Hip-hop pedagogy and the politics of identity.* New York: Teachers College.

http://inthesetimes.com/working/entry/16700/los_angeles_alex_caputo_pearl.

Hughes, S., and T. R. Berry (eds.) (2012). *The evolving significance of race: Living, learning and teaching.* New York: Peter Lang.

Incite! Women of Color Against Violence (eds.). *The revolution will not be funded: Beyond the non-profit industrial complex.* Cambridge, MA: South End.

Irizzary, J. G. (2011). *The Latinization of U.S. schools: Successful teaching and learning in shifting cultural contexts.* Boulder, CO: Paradigm.

LaRaviere, T. (May 9, 2014). Under Emmanuel, principals have no voice. *Chicago Sun-Times.*

Klinenberg, E. (2002). *Heat Wave: A social autopsy of disaster in Chicago.* London: University of Chicago.

Klonsky, M., and S. Klonsky (2008). *Small schools: Public school reform meets the ownership society.* New York: Routledge.

Koval, J. P., L. Bennett, L., M. I. J. Bennett, F. Demissie, R. Garner, and K. Kim (eds.) (2006). *The new Chicago: A social and cultural analysis.* Philadelphia: Temple University Press.

Ladson-Billings, G. (1997). Just what is critical race theory and what's it doing in a "nice" field like education. *International Journal of Qualitative Studies in Education* 11(1), 7–24.

Ladson-Billings, G. (ed.) (2003). *Critical race theory perspectives on social studies: The profession, policies, and curriculum.* Greenwich, CN: Information Age.

Ladson-Billings, G. (2006). From the achievement gap to the education debt: Understanding achievement in U.S. schools. *Educational researcher* 35(7), 3–12.

Lee, C. D., and Y. J. Majors (2003). Heading up the street: Localized opportunities for shared constructions of knowledge. *Pedagogy, culture and society* 11(3), 49–68.

Leonardo, Z. (2009). *Race, whiteness and education.* New York: Routledge.

Liou, T., and M. T. Smith (1996). The evolution and function of community development corporations in Florida's urban communities. *Housing and Society* 23(2).

Lipman, P. (2003). Chicago school policy: Regulating Black and Latino youth in the global city. *Race, Ethnicity, and Education* 6(4), 331–355.

Lipman, P. (2004). *High stakes education: Inequality, globalization, and urban school reform*. New York: Routledge.

Lipman, P. (2011). *The new political economy of urban education: Neoliberalism, race, and the right to the city*. New York: Routledge.

Lipman, P., J. Smith, E. Gutstein, and L. Dallacqua (2012, February 21). Examining CPS' plan to close, turnaround, or phase out 17 schools. *Collaborative for Equity and Justice in Education*.

Luttrel, W. (ed.) (2010). *Qualitative educational research: Readings in reflexive methodology and transformative practice*. New York: Routledge.

Lynn. M. (1999). Toward a critical race pedagogy: A research note. *Urban Education* 33(5), 606–627.

Madison, D. S. (2005). *Critical ethnography: Method, ethics, and performance*. London: Sage.

Majors, Y. J. (2007). Narrations of cross-cultural encounters as interpretive frames for reading word and world. *Discourse and Society* 18(4), 497–505.

Magallon, F. S. (2010). *Images of America: Chicago's little village Lawndale-Crawford*. Charleston, SC: Arcadia.

Metzl, J. (2009). *The protest psychosis: How schizophrenia became a Black disease*. New York: Beacon.

Mills, C. (1997). *The racial contract*. Ithaca, NY: Cornell University Press.

Mills, C. (2003). *From class to race: Essays in White Marxism and Black radicalism*. New York: Rowman & Littlefield.

Mission and Vision. http://sj.lvlhs.org/apps/pages/?uREC_ID=147999&type=d&p REC_ID=285138.

Mitchell, D. (2003). *The right to the city: Social justice and the fight for public space*. New York: Guilford.

Nambo, C. (2004). *Chicago high school redesign initiative new schools start grant:* Request for proposals for creating small Chicago public high schools at the Little Village Campus.

North, C. (2009). *Teaching for social justice? Voices from the frontlines*. Boulder, CO: Paradigm.

Oakes, J., and J. Rogers (2006). *Learning power: Organizing for education and justice*. New York: Teachers College.

Ocejo, R. (ed.) (2013). *Ethnography and the city: Readings on doing urban fieldwork*. New York: Routledge.

Olivio, A. (2004, September 22). New CHA housing is tied to jobs: Adults must work 30 hours a week. *Chicago Tribune*.

Olszewski, L., and C. Sadovi (2003, December 19). Rebirth of schools set for south side CHA and a-list of institutions have big plans. *Chicago Tribune*.

Olszewki, L. (2004, June 4). 10 city schools targeted to close: Low enrollment, building condition used as criteria. *Chicago Tribune.*

Pedroni, T. (2007). *Market movements: African-American involvement in school voucher reform.* New York: Routledge.

Popkin, S., B. Katz, M. Cunningham, K. Brown, J. Gustafson, and M. Turner (2004). A decade of HOPE VI: Research findings and policy challenges. Washington, DC: The Urban Institute and the Brookings Institution.

Prashad, V. (2007). *The darker nations: A people's history of the third world.* New York: New Press.

Rethinking Schools (2005, Summer). The small schools express, 4–6.

Rossi, R. (2012, January 27). Minister in rent-a-protester flap offers to open his books. *Chicago Sun-Times.*

Satter, B. (2009). *Family properties: How the struggle over race and real estate transformed Chicago and urban America.* New York: Holt.

Schmich, M. (2004, July 18). Dream faces bumpy road: Future as mixed-income community may pass some neighbors by. *Chicago Tribune.*

Shubert, W. (1997). *Curriculum: Perspective, paradigm and possibility.* Upper Saddle River, NJ: Prentice-Hall.

Smith, J., and D. Stovall (2008). Coming home to new homes and new schools: Critical race theory and the new politics of containment. *Journal of Education Policy* 23(2), 135–152.

Solozano D. (1997). Images and words that wound: Critical race theory, racial stereotyping, and teacher education. *Teacher Education Quarterly* 24(3), 186–215.

Stovall, D., and N. Delgado (2009). Knowing the ledge: Participatory action research as legal studies for urban high school youth. *New directions for youth development* 123, 67–82.

Stovall, D., J. Alvarado, A. Alvarez, A. Arroyo, S. Barba, G. Campos, G. Carr, et al. (2009). Getting the change we need: From a social justice high school. *Real Worlds: Student and Teacher Dialogue on Diversity and Community* 1(3):13–15.

Su, C. (2007). Cracking silent codes: Critical race theory and education organizing. *Discourse: Studies in the Cultural Politics of Education* 28(4), 531–548.

Sudbury, J., and M. Okazawa-Bey (eds.) (2009). *Activist scholarship: Antiracism, feminism and social change.* Boulder, CO: Paradigm.

Tate, W. (1997). Critical race theory and education: History, theory and implications. *Review of Research in Education* 22:195–247.

Taylor, S., F. Rizvi, B. Lingard, and M. Henry (1997). *Educational policy and the politics of change.* New York: Routledge.

Taylor, E., D. Gillborn, and G. Ladson-Billings (eds.) (2009). *Foundations of critical race theory in education.* New York: Routledge.

Tuck, E., and K. W. Wang (2012). Decolonization is not a metaphor. *Decolonization, indigeneity, education and society* 1(1), 1–40.

Thuiwai, S. (2012). *Decolonizing methodologies: Research and indigenous peoples.* New York: Zed Books.

Valdes, F., C. McCristal, and A. Harris (eds.) (2002) *Crossroads, directions, and a new critical race theory.* Philadelphia: Temple University Press.

Vaught, S. (2011). *Racism, public schooling, and the entrenchment of White supremacy: A critical race ethnography.* Albany, NY: SUNY Press.

Watkins, W. (2001). *The White architects of Black education: Ideology and power in America, 1865–1954.* New York: Teachers College.

Winndance Twine, F. (2000). *Racing research, researching race: Methodological dilemmas in critical race studies.* New York: New York University Press.

www.coreteachers.org.

www.cps.edu/NewSchools/Pages/ONS.aspx.

www.pearson.com/about-us/education/north-america.html.

www.pureparents.org.

Yamamoto, E. (1997). Critical race praxis: Race theory and political lawyering practice in post–civil rights America. *Michigan Law Review* 95(7), 821–900.

Yamamoto, E. (1999). *Interracial justice: Conflict and reconciliation in post–civil rights America.* New York: New York University Press.

Yosso, T. (2005). Whose culture has capital? A critical race theory discussion of community cultural wealth. *Race, ethnicity and education* 8(1), 69–91.

Yosso, T. (2006). *Critical race counterstories along the Chicana/Chicano educational pipeline.* New York: Routledge.

Zamundio, M. M., C. Russell, F. Rios, and J. L. Bridgeman (2011). *Critical race theory matters: Education and ideology.* New York: Routledge.

Zizek, Z. (2011). *Living in the end times.* New York: Verso.

Zuberi, T. and E. Bonilla-Silva (eds.) (2008). *White logic, White methods: Racism and Methodology.* New York: Rowman and Littlefield.

Index